The Working Railway

Approaching Borwick station, on the Wennington-Carnforth line, is Stanier 5MT 4-6-0 No 45196, in charge of the 8am Skipton-Carnforth goods on May 25 1964. One of a class of 842 locomotives which saw service all over the country, No. 45196 was ordered by the LMS in December 1934 as part of Lot No. 124, a batch of 100 engines delivered by Armstrong Whitworth in 1935. No. 45196 was withdrawn from service 33 years later, in December 1967. It was destroyed for scrap at Ward's yard, Sheffield, in March 1968.

The Working Railway

A railwayman's photographs, 1960-67

Ron Herbert

Silver Link Publishing Ltd

First published in November 1984 and April 1986 in two paperback volumes
This combined hardback edition first published December 1992

British Library Cataloguing in Publication Data

A catalogue record for this book is available from the British Library

ISBN 1 85794 000 8

Silver Link Publishing Ltd
Unit 5, Home Farm Close
Church Street
Wadenhoe
Peterborough PE8 5TE
Tel/fax (08015) 4-4-0

Printed and bound in Great Britain

To Preston Control, which closed on May 12 1985. When the telephone rang, a controller could always tell if trouble was on the way, just by the tone of the caller's voice. 'Hello control . . .' May the words long be remembered!

Left: Riddles 'Britannia' Pacific No 70052 *Firth of Tay* forges up the bank south of Lancaster with a Glasgow Central-Euston relief (1X77) on July 6 1963.

Right: A magnificent sight indeed. The up 'Royal Scot' is hurried south over the River Lune and into Lancaster Castle station on March 15 1961, behind Stanier 'Princess Coronation' class 8P 'Pacific' No 46247 *City of Liverpool*, then allocated to Carlisle Kingmoor shed (12A). This locomotive, which entered traffic in September 1943 as a streamlined locomotive carrying plain wartime black livery, lost its streamlined casings and gained smoke deflectors in May 1947. It survived until June 1963, when it was withdrawn after covering 1,388,187 miles in service - an average of nearly 70,000 miles a year since it entered traffic. It was broken up for scrap at Crewe Works in July 1963.

Contents

Acknowledgements

Putting together the two original volumes of photographs was a thoroughly enjoyable task and prompted many happy memories both of my work and my railway photography. Although my name appears on this book, it would never have appeared without the help and support of many people, and I would like to acknowledge their assistance here.

First of all I would like to thank my colleagues on the railway past and present - especially those in Control - for their professional expertise and help. Without the invaluable aid of my friends in Traffic Control in particular, some of the pictures which follow simply would not have been possible.

My thanks also to my wife Christine, for putting up with the piles of pictures, timetables and books involved in the business of editing and caption writing. Whilst writing the captions I was appreciative of the help given by Peter Smith, formerly a locomotive driver on the Somerset & Dorset line: his help in captioning my 'S&D' photographs produced some interesting detail.

I would also like to say a hearty word of thanks to Derek Mercer for producing such outstanding prints from my negatives, many of which were then 20 years old.

Finally my sincere thanks to Jayne and Nigel Harris, the original proprietors of Silver Link Publishing Ltd, for all the help and encouragement in guiding me through the business of compiling the original volumes - a new experience for me - and for aiming at the highest quality at every stage.

My pictures have given me a great deal of pleasure over the years and I'm pleased to be able to share them once more in this new combined hardback edition.

Lancaster Castle station, where I started work for BR training as a Telegraph Clerk on April 21 1958, was always a superb location for photographing steam - and it offered a host of varied vantage points. This was the view from the south end of the down platform on April 15 1961 as Stanier 'Black 5' 4-6-0 No 45244, of Carlisle Upperby shed (12B), rattled through on the up fast line with the 9.50am Carlisle-Warrington freight.

Introduction

I am more than pleased to write this Introduction to the new combined edition of Volumes 1 and 2 of *The Working Railway*. When Will Adams of Silver Link told me they wished to reprint both volumes in a combined hardback book I was, to say the least, pleased. I have combined the two Introductions, and I hope that this will convey something of the railway as it was during the period 1960-67, a period that brought much satisfaction to me as a railwayman.

It's a common enough saying that railways are 'in the blood' but it was certainly true in my case, for my father was not only a professional railwayman but also a knowledgeable railway enthusiast. His interest in railways was very deep indeed and he never went anywhere without his much-thumbed copy of the 'Bradshaw' timetable.

I suppose it was therefore inevitable that this interest would rub off, and sure enough it did. I can well recall childhood holidays which were always taken at a location which could be classed as a holiday centre - but which, more importantly, was a railway centre of great interest. From my father's base, then at Chester, we travelled in the 1950s to Scarborough, Gourock, Bournemouth and Bangor (County Down), all of which seemed to me at the time to be far-away places!

One of my first memories of such a holiday was travelling from Prestatyn, our home, to Heysham Harbour in the summer of 1950 to join the SS *Duke of Lancaster* for the night sailing to Belfast, en route to Bangor. We left Belfast Queens Quay the following morning behind a B&CDR 4-4-2T, the first of many steam-hauled runs in Northern Ireland which were to extend through to the late 1960s. These were some of my happiest days in pursuit of steam traction with my companions and camera. There is no doubt that this early introduction to Irish railways prompted me to make the crossing of the Irish Sea on numerous occasions for the next 17 years. It was a marvellous system - a superb example of the working railway of the steam era.

In 1953 my father was transferred from Chester to Carnforth as a Relief Station Master, covering the area from Leyland to Penrith, and including the Windermere and Keswick branches. This was the turning point in my growing interest in railways, for having been used to the smooth running of steam on the North Wales Coast, or the sight of trains ambling down the many branches in the area, I was suddenly plunged into a railway full of Anglo-Scottish expresses hauled by majestic Stanier Class 8P Pacifics, 'Britannia' Pacifics, 'Royal Scot' and 'Patriot' 4-6-0s, unlimited numbers (it seemed!) of Stanier 'Black 5s' - also Riddles 'Clan' Pacifics which always appeared to have a Fowler Class 2 4-4-0 attached in front as a pilot engine!

Every time you approached Carnforth station the up and down loops would be full of freight trains awaiting train crew relief or a path onto the main line behind one of the many passenger trains. It was a busy, bustling scene which drew me like a magnet and it was then that I realised that I wanted to be a part of this working railway when I left school.

At last, on April 21 1958 I began my railway career on British Railways at Lancaster Castle station, training as a telegraph clerk. It is hard to believe as I look back to those days that all telegrams and train reporting was conducted in morse code, devices such as teleprinters being unheard of at Lancaster! Part of the duties of the Telegraph section was to report to the Control at Preston, who would be informed of the passing times of trains at selected locations. This was my first contact with Control and, like my colleagues, I treated them with the greatest respect. I was at last part of the working railway and I was enjoying every minute of it. I also became much more aware of the details of train working, and in February 1960 I bought a Zeiss Werra 35 mm camera so I could begin to record the everyday scene as I saw it operate. Thus began my serious railway photography, which was to continue for the next seven years.

In May of that year I travelled on a Manchester Locomotive Society/Stephenson Locomotive Society railtour from Lancaster Castle to Glasson Dock and then on to Penrith via Lancaster Castle, Green Ayre,

Clapham, Ingleton and Shap. We then continued to Kirkby Stephen East via Appleby East and returned to Lancaster Castle via Ravenstonedale, Tebay, Arnside, Ulverston and the Lakeside branch. Looking at the railway map of today, bearing this route in mind, is a revealing exercise.

In June I made the first of many visits to the Isle of Man. Runs over the complete network to Peel, Port Erin and Ramsay were all achieved, including a visit to Douglas shed and works, where enthusiasts were not normally welcome. The IOMR was an idyllic scene, especially for the railway photographer, and I went back many times.

During 1961 many trips were arranged on lines long since closed, such as the Peterhead and Fraserburgh branches and the St Combs Light Railway, steam to Ballachulish, Brecon to Neath, Bath Green Park to Templecombe, the Fowey and Helston branches, Bodmin Road to Wadebridge, Bude, and Halwill Junction to Barnstaple via the Torrington Light Railway. I also made the first of many visits to the Isle of Wight, which featured a superb largely Victorian steam-worked railway. The latter part of the summer saw a visit to north and central Wales, photographing the narrow gauge lines, and, more importantly, steam on the Cambrian. August brought a further highlight with the MLS/SLS 'Furness Railtour' which ran over many lines long since closed to passengers at the time; the North Lonsdale branch, Dalton to Stainton Quarry, Ormsgill Junction to Buccleuch Dock, Barrow shipyard station, the Hodbarrow branch from Millom, and the beautiful Coniston branch from Foxfield.

In March of 1962 a most important change took place in my railway career. I was summoned to Preston to be interviewed by the District Operating Superintendent and some days later I was advised that I would shortly be transferred to Traffic Control and start training as an Assistant Controller. So began my Control career, which was to continue for many years. I soon became aware that 'the Control' was the focal point of all train operation in the area and with the aid of my new colleagues I was soon being advised which locomotives were working specific trains, and of any unusual movements that were being arranged - official or otherwise! Consequently my Zeiss Werra became standard equipment to take to work, as the

opportunities were endless and extremely varied. Control was an exacting but incredibly satisfying job and I look back very happily on this period. Each shift brought its share of crises and emergencies, but this ensured lots of interest, and gave the individual the chance to prove his ability. It was a job of great professionalism and friendly comradeship with your colleagues. Control was the hub of railway operation and required maximum concentration and commitment, but it was not without its lighter moments. At this time Beeching's cuts were fast approaching and the main holiday that summer was spent photographing the remaining 'King' 4-6-0s on Hatton bank, in addition to the Bulleid Pacifics on the Waterloo-Salisbury-Bournemouth lines. Some time was spent on the S&DJR line and on the last day of our tour we visited Bromsgrove, at the foot of the Lickey Incline. Happy days. Once again, a railtour completed a most successful year. It was organised by the Railway Correspondence & Travel Society and began at the Fishergate Hill station, in Preston, and ran to Grassington via Longridge, Padiham and Colne, and returning via Blackburn, Cherry Tree and Chorley.

The Modernisation Plan had not had much impact upon the day-to-day operating practices and appearances of the railway network of the North West. In other parts of the country modernisation was proceeding at an ever-increasing rate, but apart from the limited introduction of a few diesel-electric locomotives and diesel multiple units, railway life and business in the North West continued more or less exactly as it had done for decades. Freight trains continued to serve the local branch lines to Longridge, Pilling, Preston Fishergate Hill and Preston Dock, which was still extremely busy and operated its own fleet of steam locomotives. BR provided a pair of 350 hp 0-6-0 diesel shunters (today's Class 08) to work traffic in and out of the Dock Authority's sidings to marshalling yards at Bamber Bridge, Lostock Hall, Farington, Ribble Sidings and North Union Sidings. Furthermore, this traffic ran 24 hours a day!

Passenger trains worked by steam locomotives continued to run between Preston, Southport, Blackpool and Fleetwood. At Blackpool Central station 14 platforms were worked to capacity during the frequently chaotic summer months. It seemed at the time that it would never - could never - change. The Modernisation Plan of 1955 still appeared to be something which people talked about, but which did little to affect railway activities and business in our area. We were on the brink of tremendous change, however.

It became clearly apparent that things were about to change radically with the introduction of the plan to 'reshape' Britain's railways under Dr Richard Beeching, in 1963. This plan eliminated virtually at a stroke much of the railway environment featured in these pages. Not only was the steam locomotive itself doomed, but signal boxes were closed and torn down, whole track layouts were simplified and once-common items like line-side telegraph poles have today all but disappeared.

Many of the traditional operating practices survived, however, and unofficial train titles were in everyday use by signalmen and Controllers. They never appeared in any timetable, but there was the 'Horse & Carriage', officially 3K16, the 8.15am Carlisle-Crewe parcels; the 'Morning Star', the 4.30am freight from Carlisle to Carnforth, and the 'Pilling Pig', the 2.45pm freight from Pilling to Preston North Union. Other common everyday titles were 'The Biscuits', which was the 6.42pm freight from Blackpool North to Crewe, the 'Box Vans', officially the 7.15am Corkickle-St Helens freight, and the 'Quix', which was the 8.44am freight from Hunslet to Heysham Harbour. A particularly descriptive example was the 6.40pm freight from Carlton to Carnforth, known throughout the area as the 'Creeping Death'! There were many others.

1963 began with interesting train movements in the Lancaster & Morecambe area caused by the reconstruction of Lune Bridge ('Carlisle Bridge') at Lancaster, and for two weekends the main-line services were diverted via Bare Lane, Morecambe, Lancaster Green Ayre and via the steep single line to Lancaster Castle. It was a photographer's dream come true. In July I changed my long-serving Werra for a Rolleicord, armed with which I made further visits to Northern Ireland, the Isle of Wight and the Isle of Man to complete another successful year in search of steam.

During 1963 Carlisle Marshalling Yard was

brought into use and life began to change. In the Beeching report, the line from Poulton to Blackpool North was recommended for closure, which, although a sad loss, appeared logical, bearing in mind that the large terminus at Blackpool Central was served by the busy coastal route. We were amazed to learn in 1964 that Blackpool Central was to close and that Blackpool North would survive, while the coastal route serving Central would terminate at Blackpool South, on the outskirts of the town. Things changed with a vengeance - Blackpool Central closed in November 1964 and the site was sold to become a car park and bingo hall. The Marton line, the direct link from Kirkham to Blackpool South, closed in 1967, when Fleetwood also closed, its line being cut back to Wyre Dock. The Pilling branch was cut back to Garstang Town in 1963 and closed completely two years later.

The line from Preston to Southport also disappeared in 1964, with the branches to Glasson Dock, Longridge and Low Gill-Clapham Junction all going the same way as time passed. The beautiful 'little North Western' line from Wennington Junction to Morecambe closed in January 1966, as did Lancaster Green Ayre shed, one of my favourite haunts. It was a period of rapid change, closures and withdrawals and there was so little time to try and record it all. Things would never be the same again.

As I think back to the arrival of the first English Electric Type 4s, which displaced the Stanier Pacifics from the Anglo-Scottish expresses, I also recall the stranger sights we saw like the North British diesel-hydraulics passing Castle station in ex-works condition, en route from the NB works at Glasgow for commissioning on the Western Region. Little did we think that the hydraulics would have such a short lifespan, unlike the 'EE4', which commanded much popularity at the end of their long lives amongst the enthusiast fraternity.

Amongst the photographs are a number taken in Scotland during the limited period of operation of the four-wheeled diesel railbuses. These arrived too late to make any significant impact but I was fortunate to travel on one of these vehicles from Aviemore to Elgin in 1961, and from Gleneagles to Comrie in 1962. Alas, both the railbuses and their lines have gone for ever from the BR network. Also long-gone into history is Inverurie works, which appears in this book.

At the beginning of 1964 I changed my camera again, this time buying a Rolleiflex, and in March I photographed Fowler 2-6-4T No 42301 at Glasson Dock, en route to the local shipbreakers yard for cutting up. This was the only occasion a locomotive was cut up at Glasson Dock. A visit to Northern Ireland followed which included a footplate trip over the border to Dundalk on a Class WT 2-6-4T. In May I returned home and spent as much time as I could at the trackside on the branch lines, which Beeching was now closing so quickly that it was impossible to get to many of them in time.

May also brought Riddles 'Clan' Pacific No 72007 *Clan Mackintosh* to Lancaster Penny Street station on the RCTS 'Ribble Lune' railtour - a sight never to be forgotten. Another RCTS railtour took place on the Glasson Dock branch during June, when an Ivatt 2MT 2-6-0 hauled a train of brake vans over its five-mile length.

September 1964 brought the fateful day when No 46256 *Sir William A. Stanier FRS* worked its last day in service on the RCTS 'Scottish Lowlander' railtour and thus brought the era of the Stanier Pacifics on the WCML to an end. It was a sad day and I realised the end was near. In 1965 I therefore travelled north to see the Gresley A4 Pacifics on the Aberdeen-Glasgow services - another never-to-be-forgotten sight.

In May of 1965 I went to France to see SNCF steam in action between Calais and Amiens, followed by a trip to another old favourite, the Romney, Hythe & Dymchurch Railway. Before the end of the year I managed to fit in a trip to Germany to see DB steam at work, and squeezed in shed visits to Munich, Mannheim, Stuttgart and Koblenze.

Time was running out fast in 1966 and it was a case of trying to fit in as much as possible before the end came. It was a time of 'last days' and 'last trains' as lines, stations and sheds closed and steam steadily faded away in grime and neglect. The year's highlights included visits to the Isle of Wight, a high-speed run behind an A4 between Glasgow and Aberdeen, and a trip to Bournemouth and Weymouth to pay homage to the Bulleid Pacifics, while autumn brought a holiday in Eire, returning home via Belfast and Larne in order to photograph the remaining Class WT 2-6-4Ts.

1967 was the end, and with my Rollei I began my last year of railway photography. January took me to Sicily to see the remaining FS steam locomotives, while in May I was back to Northern Ireland to photograph the WT 2-6-4T No 10 and GSR 0-6-0 No 186 on a Railway Preservation Society of Ireland special on the Portrush branch. Numerous trips to Bournemouth and Weymouth continued until the fateful day of 8 July, when Southern Steam breathed its last on BR metals. September witnessed a visit to Spain and Portugal to see what was left of RENFE and CP's once large fleet of steam locomotives, by then much depleted.

As I say in this book, operationally in Britain steam had become a real liability, and for Traffic Control August 1968 saw an end to the endless stream of failures, late running and other operating disasters which had been caused by the neglected and run-down engines. The end of steam was a release from a good deal of difficulty in this respect, but it also drew the fires on a period which for me had been a very interesting and photographically rewarding era of the working railway. It was an experience I shall never forget, and I hope the following pictures will convey some of the unique appeal of the working railway. They have certainly rekindled many happy memories for me!

It seems a long time ago indeed that we covered the country to stand at the trackside photographing BR's steam fleet. One of my companions from those days persistently refused to point his camera at a mere Stanier 5MT 4-6-0, claiming that there were just too many of them about. How times change!

Ron Herbert
Preston
Lancashire

Part 1

Stanier 8F 2-8-0 No 48319 hauls an engineers special from Heysham tip to Northampton across the level crossing at Bare Lane, Morecambe, at 11am on January 24 1964. I didn't have to go far to take pictures like this, as my father was Station Master at Bare Lane and I lived there from 1956 until 1971. My interest in railways must have sprung from my father's dedication to and enthusiasm for his job.

LANCASTER

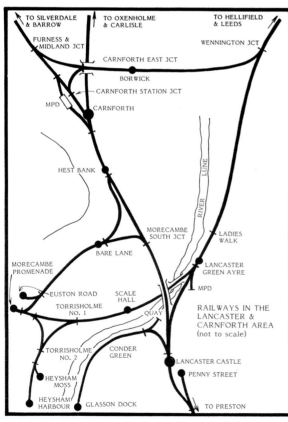

TO SILVERDALE & BARROW

TO OXENHOLME & CARLISLE

TO HELLIFIELD & LEEDS

FURNESS & MIDLAND JCT

WENNINGTON JCT

CARNFORTH EAST JCT

BORWICK

CARNFORTH STATION JCT

MPD

CARNFORTH

HEST BANK

RIVER LUNE

MORECAMBE SOUTH JCT

LADIES WALK

BARE LANE

MORECAMBE PROMENADE

LANCASTER GREEN AYRE

EUSTON ROAD

SCALE HALL

MPD

TORRISHOLME NO. 1

QUAY

RAILWAYS IN THE LANCASTER & CARNFORTH AREA (not to scale)

TORRISHOLME NO. 2

CONDER GREEN

LANCASTER CASTLE

PENNY STREET

HEYSHAM MOSS

HEYSHAM HARBOUR

GLASSON DOCK

TO PRESTON

Above: A railway location which no longer exists — Lancaster Penny Street station. This was the original Lancaster & Preston Railway station, which closed to passengers in 1849, but which remained open for freight until the mid-1960s. This train was the RCTS Ribble-Lune railtour, hauled by Riddles 'Clan' Pacific No. 72007 Clan Mackintosh, **on May 23 1964**

Right: Looking south from Lancaster No. 2 signalbox on April 23 1965. Riddles Class 7P6F No. 70034 Thomas Hardy **coasts down the bank towards Lancaster Castle station with 1L25 — the 10.10am Euston-Carlisle, composed entirely of Mk. 1 stock. This section today comprises a double-track section with an up goods loop.**

Left: A southbound Lancaster departure, viewed from the up side of the WCML. Stanier 'Jubilee' 4-6-0 No. 45582 *Central Provinces* heads the 10.35am Carnforth-Warrington freight of June 8 1962. This turn could provide almost anything in the way of motive power.

Above: 'The Duke' at Lancaster. Sole Riddles 8P Pacific No. 71000 *Duke of Gloucester* **gets to grips with the southbound climb from Lancaster Castle on February 17 1962 with 3K16, the 8.15am Carlisle-Crewe, known locally as 'The Horse & Carriage.' A sighting of No. 71000 on this section at this time was very rare. The vehicle immediately behind the tender is a Gresley BG.**

Riddles Caprotti Class 5 4-6-0 No. 73129, of Patricroft shed, shunts at Lancaster with the 11.42am Milnthorpe-Bay Horse freight of February 7 1962. This locomotive, built in 1956, is now being restored at the Midland Railway Centre, Butterley.

Top: Waiting for the rightaway at Lancaster Castle on March 13 1962 are light-engines (left) Ivatt 4MT 2-6-0 No. 43124 and Ivatt 2MT 2-6-0 No. 46422. The Class 4MT had arrived with the 8.15am parcels from Heysham. The 'live wires' sign to the right refers to the catenary of the Lancaster-Morecambe-Heysham electrified section, which started under the bridge.

Above: Stanier Class 8P Pacific No. 46222 *Queen Mary* comes off the fast line at Lancaster No. 2 signalbox with the 10.5am Glasgow-Birmingham (IM24) of February 7 1962. The up yard behind the 'Pacific' survived in considerably truncated form until summer 1984.

Right: No. 46229 *Duchess of Hamilton*, now preserved in working order at the National Railway Museum, York, stands at Lancaster Castle on March 16 1962 at the head of the 12.20pm Perth-Euston (1M37).

Below: A pre-grouping image at Lancaster Castle, as LNWR 'Super D' 0-8-0 No. 49428 ambles north on the down fast line with the 6.25am Ribble Sidings-Heysham Harbour freight, March 19 1961. The building behind the engine is the original Lancaster & Carlisle Railway station of 1849.

This is one of my favourite Stanier Class 8P photographs. No. 46234 *Duchess of Abercorn* passes Lancaster No. 3 signalbox with 2K82 — the 6.20am Carlisle-Crewe — of August 1 1961.

The 3.15pm Windermere-Liverpool Exchange (1K47) of August 5 1961 rolls into Lancaster Castle behind Caprotti 'Black 5' No. 44745. Note the three non-corridor coaches marshalled behind the engine and the marvellous gas lamp on the bridge, above the locomotive.

The northward view from Lancaster No. 4 signalbox on August 12 1961, as 'Princess Royal' 4-6-2 No. 46206 *Princess Marie Louise* prepares for the assault on Lancaster bank with the 10am Glasgow-Euston (1M25). A 'Princess Royal' on this train was most unusual.

This was a superb vantage point — looking south from Lancaster No. 4 and I was particularly pleased with this photograph. Rebuilt 'Patriot' 4-6-0 No. 45522 *Prestatyn* leaves Lancaster with the 1.30pm Manchester Victoria-Glasgow of March 22 1963. The leading coaches are all LMS vehicles. Waiting in No. 2 bay is a Lancaster Green Ayre 2-6-4T with a local service for Morecambe.

Right: A northbound departure from Lancaster Castle, as seen from the up side of the line. With a pair of horseboxes behind the tender No. 46247 *City of Liverpool* **gets under way with the 9.20am Crewe-Perth (1S53) on March 15 1962.**

Another view south from the lofty Lancaster No. 4 signalbox. Stanier's first 'Pacific' No. 46200 *The Princess Royal* hurries north on the down fast line through Castle station at the head of the 10.5am Euston-Perth (1S63) on March 16 1962. The line diverging to the right over the diamond crossing went to Glasson dock, whilst the branch on the left was the electrified Midland line to Green Ayre.

Above: Stanier 8F 2-8-0 No. 48711, coupled to a narrow-sided Fowler tender, passes Lancaster on the down fast line with a 'Covhop' train — the 1.10pm Burn Naze-Corkickle of June 20 1964. 'Covhop' was the official description of a 'covered hopper.'

Below: The impressive view from the base of Lancaster No. 4 on June 8 1964, with Stanier Class 8P No. 46238 *City of Carlisle* leaving on the 2.54pm Preston-Barrow (1L21). The unusual appearance of a 'Duchess' on a Barrow train was arranged by Preston control . . .

Above: The double-track main line across Lancaster's Lune Bridge (known as Carlisle Bridge) was interlaced during reconstruction work in 1963 to give the civil engineering gang working clearances. No. 45317 treads cautiously over the bridge with the 1pm Carlisle-Warrington fast freight on February 26. Close inspection of the picture reveals the interlaced rails, which give the appearance of single track.

Reconstruction of the bridge opened up this new photographic location for a short period. 'Jubilee' 4-6-0 No. 45592 *Indore* crosses the Lune with the 5.10pm Manchester Exchange-Windermere (1L32) of July 25. Reconstruction involved the provision of a new deck on the original piers.

'Crab' 2-6-0 No. 42838 prepares to cross the River Lune over the Greyhound Bridge, from Lancaster Green Ayre station, with the 10.47am Leeds Morecambe of August 22 1961. Approaching Green Ayre from Morecambe is EMU No. M29024M. The 10mph speed restriction, uphill climb and sharp curve of this line from Green Ayre was a real test for drivers. This bridge now carries Lancaster's main road to the north.

Above: A very rare sighting at Lancaster Green Ayre during the afternoon of August 31 1962, as Class O4/8 2-8-0 No. 63837 of Immingham shed (40B) passes with the 8am special freight from Immingham to Heysham Moss. Once again, my thanks to the Control staff for making the necessary arrangements! Green Ayre station closed on January 3 1966.

Right: Approaching Scale Hall station on January 24 1964 is Fowler 4F 0-6-0 No. 44570 on the 12.40pm Heysham Moss-Tees ICI freight. The catenary equipment was the test section for BR's 25kv system. This stretch was known as 'The Golden Mile' because of the different types of experimental masts tested, as evident in this picture.

Above: The Midland line from Green Ayre to Morecambe Promenade, as seen from Carlisle bridge. EMU No. M28220M approaches Greyhound Bridge with the 2.10pm Morecambe-Lancaster Castle, January 24 1964. This trackbed is now a road.

Everything in this photograph has now gone. EMU No. 29023 pauses at Scale Hall station, between Morecambe Promenade and Lancaster, with the 12.40pm Morecambe-Lancaster Castle of September 23 1964. This station, opened by BR on June 8 1957 and closed in the Beeching plan on January 3 1966, must have been one of the shortest-lived on the railway.

Right: Once again, a railway scene which exists now in memory only. 'Crab' 2-6-0 No. 42888 marshalls the 11.13am Ladies Walk-Manvers Main Colliery empties at Ladies Walk Sidings, Lancaster on August 1 1963. This line was closed on January 3 1966 and this site is now occupied by small industrial units.

A view of New Zealand sidings from Skerton Bridge, Lancaster, June 30 1963. LMS 'Jinty' 0-6-0T No. 47651 approaches Green Ayre station with the 2.37pm Trip No. 72 to Lancaster Castle. Four other locomotives are visible. All you can see from here today is trees.

Above: To see this location today you would hardly believe this railway existed. Stanier 'Jubilee' 4-6-0 No. 45564 *New South Wales* passes New Zealand Sidings (left) and Ladies Walk Sidings (right) with the four-coach 7.17pm Morecambe Promenade-Leeds (2N71) of July 30 1963.

Left: Stanier 'Black 5' 4-6-0 No. 44672 leaves Ladies Walk en-route to Leeds with the 2.46pm from Morecambe Promenade (2N71) of June 15 1963. The train is seen running behind Lancaster's Lansil factory.

THE GLASSON DOCK BRANCH

Above: Lancaster's other branch linked the WCML with the city's own quay and also with Glasson Dock at the mouth of the River Lune. Ivatt 2MT 2-6-0 No. 46422 shunts empty vans into Williamson's factory on Lancaster quay on March 11 1964.

Above: No. 46422 propels withdrawn Fowler 2-6-4T No. 42301 into the shipbreakers scrapyard at Glasson Dock, five miles from Lancaster, on March 11 1964. Opened in 1878, the Glasson Dock branch closed to passengers at this tiny station on July 5 1930, and closed completely on September 7 1964.

This RCTS brake-van special traversed the five-mile Glasson Dock branch on June 20 1964, hauled by Ivatt 2MT 2-6-0 No. 46433, seen here passing Conder Green. The train comprises four BR and two LMS 20-ton brake vans, weighing 120 tons in all.

Left: This was a very unusual occurrence at Glasson Dock. Ivatt No. 46422 propels five-plank wagons of nitro-chalk from Heysham Moss onto the quay for shipment, March 2 1962. The floating cafe in the canal basin on the left is still in operation today.

Ivatt 2MT 2-6-0 No. 46422 runs cautiously over the weed covered track at Glasson Dock on March 2 1962, after working a train of nitro-chalk to the quay, for shipment. (See page 25). In the background stands the sailing ship *Moby Dick*, which was eventually destroyed by fire at Morecambe.

NORTH OF LANCASTER

A Stanier Class 8P in full cry. With a clear exhaust, No. 46250 *City of Lichfield* speeds north towards Morecambe South Junction with 'The Lakes Express' (1L27) of August 31 1963. The 'Duchess' was accelerating away from a stop at Lancaster.

Joining the WCML at Morecambe South Junction on June 3 1961 is grimy 'Black 5' No. 45427, of Carnforth shed (24L), with the 4.55pm non-corridor Morecambe Euston Road-Lancaster Castle.

Above: A wide variety of traffic and motive power was always on offer at Morecambe South Junction — and freight traffic was intense. 'Patriot' 4-6-0 No. 45501 *St Dunstan's* steams south on June 3 1961 with the 8.47am Carlisle-Ince Moss freight.

Stanier 2-8-0 No. 48386 awaits assistance between Bare Lane and Morecambe South Junction after stalling with 4P20 — the 6.12pm Heysham Moss-Darwen oil train, May 9 1967 'Black 5' No. 45450 arrived to assist the train, which weighed more than 700 tons.

Above: 'Black 5' No. 45448 blasts up the 1 in 100 incline from Bare Lane to Morecambe South Junction with the 3.10pm Heysham Harbour-Farington freight of February 5 1962.

Below: Viewed from Morecambe South Junction signal box, 5MT No. 45197 heads north with 'The Royal Scot' (9.5am Euston-Glasgow) on February 5 1962, in place of a failed EE Type 4 diesel.

HEST BANK

Above: As might be expected, the ubiquitous 'Black 5' could turn up on just about any duty. On May 28 1960 Carnforth's No. 44709 works the 1pm Workington-Manchester Victoria, at Hest Bank.

The West Coast Main Line at Hest Bank was a superb location to see trains running at high speeds. In this view, grubby Riddles 'Britannia' No. 70019 *Lightning* heads south with meat for Smithfield Market — the 1pm Carlisle-Broad Street of September 15 1963 (4A08).

Above: This is one of my favourite pictures, taken in a little-photographed location. 'Crab' 2-6-0 No. 42836 hurries south at Hest Bank with an up relief on August 1 1960.

Left: Hest Bank again, this time on July 6 1963. Fowler 2-6-4T No. 42319, at the head of a rake of LMS stock, steams south with the 3.15pm Windermere - Liverpool Exchange (1K47).

Right: 'Patriot' 4-6-0s became more common on the WCML in this area after 1965, when a batch were transferred to Lancaster Green Ayre (24J). On October 10 1961 No. 45510 races south at Hest Bank with the 10.30 Carlisle-Red Bank.

Below: Riddles 'Britannia' Pacific No. 70052 *Firth of Tay*, coupled to a BRID high capacity tender speeds past Hest Bank with the 10.50am Glasgow-Manchester Victoria of June 18 1961.

Above: The aftermath of the major mishap of May 20 1965, when the 10.10pm Glasgow-Kensington (1V42) was derailed at Hest Bank. Stanier 8F 2-8-0 No. 48199 marshalls damaged sleeping cars in readiness for transfer to Morecambe Balloon Carriage Sidings, on June 21 1965..

Left: Hest Bank station on July 13 1964. Leaving the up platform is Riddles 4MT 4-6-0 No. 75048 with the seven-coach 3.15pm Windermere - Liverpool Exchange (1K47). No. 75048 was allocated to Bank Hall, Liverpool at this time.

Above: A busy spell at Hest Bank station on October 3 1964, as Carnforth shed's Fowler 2-6-4T No. 42322 pauses with the 3.15pm Windermere Town-Lancaster (2P83). This station closed to passengers on February 3 1969, though the signal box, just visible beyond the footbridge, survives as a level crossing frame.

'Britannia' No. 70042 Lord Roberts sprints through Hest Bank station, working the 9.53pm Willesden-Carlisle parcels of March 4 1965. The 20-ton goods brake van in the middle of the train was provided for the guard as it was equipped with a coal-burning stove. The rear vehicle is a Gresley BG. Although closed in 1969, the station platforms survived until electrification of the WCML in the early 1970s.

Above: Hest Bank is the only place on the 401¼-mile London-Glasgow West Coast Main Line where the railway actually runs next to the sea — and only then for about ¼-mile! Here we see Stanier 'Mogul' No. 42945 on the seaside stretch with the 6am Carlisle-Bescot mixed of June 20 1961. The left-hand track gives access to Morecambe for southbound WCML trains, from a crossover and junction at Hest Bank station.

The single line connection from Hest Bank to Bare Lane forms a triangle with the WCML (seen in the background) and the Bare Lane-Morecambe South Junction double track section. Running from Hest Bank towards Bare Lane on June 23 1964 are 'Jinty' 0-6-0Ts Nos. 47599 and 47616 (both from Carnforth shed) on the 2.30pm Carnforth-Heysham Harbour (T84). The train is largely made up of 'Oxfit' cattle wagons for the Harbour and ICI tank wagons for Heysham Moss.

BARE LANE
MORECAMBE

Above: Outside the peak holiday periods the *TSS Duke of Lancaster*, which plied mainly between Heysham and Belfast, was used as a cruise ship to the Scottish isles, Scandinavia and Portugal. Trains connecting with these services ran from London, and in this view Stanier 'Jubilee' 4-6-0 No. 45613 *Kenya* hauls a return Holiday Cruise special from Heysham Harbour to Euston at Bare Lane, Morecambe, on May 28 1963.

Relaying the up main line at Bare Lane: snowplough-fitted Lancaster-Green Ayre 'Austerity' 2-8-0 No. 90706 propels engineers ballast wagons over the newly laid track on March 26 1961.

Morecambe versus Chester: 'Jubilee' No. 45696 *Arethusa* — with Fowler tender — storms through Bare Lane with a football special en route to Chester on December 8 1961. The seaside town could not resist advertising its attractions on the 'Jubilee's' smokebox door!

41

Top: Coupled to a motley selection of rolling stock, unrebuilt 'Patriot' 4-6-0 No. 45513 waits near Bare Lane for acceptance onto the WCML at Morecambe South Junction, on March 5 1961, with the 9.25am Heysham Harbour to Manchester Victoria parcels. The single line to the right is the connection from Bare Lane to Hest Bank.

Above: Collecting the single line token at Bare Lane for the section to Hest Bank. 'Jinty' 0-6-0Ts Nos. 47616 and 47599 lead the 12.25 Morecambe-Carnforth freight (T84) over the level crossing adjacent to the station on June 23 1964.

Above: The view from our landing window in the station house at Bare Lane just before lunchtime on March 8 1960. Fowler 2-6-4T No. 42409 — a Leeds Holbeck engine — approaches the platforms with the 11.21am Morecambe-Carnforth freight.

Left: A sunny morning between Bare Lane and Morecambe South Junction on February 9 1963 and Ivatt 4MT 2-6-0 No. 43124, with self cleaning smokebox, runs under clear signals towards the WCML with three non-corridor coaches forming the 9.55am Morecambe Promenade to Lancaster Castle passenger.

Right: Begrimed Ivatt 2MT 2-6-0 No. 46441 — now preserved at Steamtown, Carnforth in much cleaner condition — is ready for departure from Bare Lane station with the 4.55pm ex-Lakeside 'Lake Windermere Cruise' of August 9 1965. The train is a mixture of LMS and Mk 1 stock.

MORECAMBE
EUSTON ROAD

Morecambe Euston Road was the LNWR terminus at the seaside resort and was located approximately ¾-mile short of the existing Promenade station. Euston Road closed for normal passenger services in September 1958, but remained open for summer season trains until the mid '60s. This view, on September 7 1961, shows Ivatt 4MT 2-6-0 No. 43117 with the 11.48am service to Lancaster Castle. This site is now occupied by homes for senior citizens.

Above: The Euston Road station staff and Stanier 2-6-4T No. 42589 on August 24 1961. My father, Arthur Herbert — second from the left — was Euston Road's Station Master at this time. The train was the 11.48am to Lancaster Castle.

Below: Fairburn 2-6-4T No. 42136, framed by the impressive signal gantry at Euston Road's station throat, crosses to the up main line with the three-coach non-corridor 9.55am Morecambe Promenade - Lancaster Castle of September 11 1961. This loco spent its entire life at Lancaster Green Ayre shed.

CARNFORTH

The impressive layout at Carnforth No. 1 Junction on May 14 1963 is the setting for another favourite photograph. English Electric Type 4 diesel No. D303 works south with the 6.35pm Kendal — Euston parcels 1A65. A Gresley BG is immediately behind the engine.

Above: Carlisle Kingmoor Shed's 'Black 5' No. 44669 enters the down main line platform at Carnforth on May 23 1963 at the head of the 8am additional freight to Carlisle yard. Rationalisation over the years has radically altered this scene — even the main line platforms no longer exist.

An unusual visitor to Carnforth shed (10A) on September 19 1966 was withdrawn LNER A4 Pacific No. 60026 *Miles Beevor*, en-route to Crewe Works behind Stanier 8F No. 48346. Parts of No. 60026 were used in the overhaul of No. 60007 *Sir Nigel Gresley*, following its purchase by the A4 Locomotive Society.

Above: Pre-Steamtown days at Carnforth MPD. Locomotives visible in this overall view from the top of the coaling plant are Nos. 46499, 43103, 43066, 45328 and 48536. Another group of engines are visible in Keer Sidings, at the north end of the shed. July 2 1966.

Right: It's July 2 1966 and standing on the ashpit at 10A are Stanier 5MTs Nos. 45328 and 45092, and Stanier 8F 2-8-0 No. 48556.

Dramatic lighting at the south end of Carnforth shed on September 12 1964 highlights 'Black 5' No. 45156 *Ayrshire Yeomanry* and Riddles 'Britannia' Pacific No. 70023 *Venus*.

Right: Former Carnforth Driver Ronnie 'Blackie' Nelson and Fairburn 2-6-4T No. 2073 at 10A on June 1 1969, after the end of BR steam and by which time the Fairburn had been privately purchased and restored in LNWR 'blackberry black' livery. The loco is now on the Lakeside & Haverthwaite Railway.

Below: With its chimney sacked over, snowplough-fitted Fowler 4F 0-6-0 No. 44300 awaits winter weather and a return to duty at Carnforth shed on November 15 1964.

Above: Having arrived on the down main line at Furness & Midland Junction, 'Jinty' 0-6-0Ts Nos. 47375 and 47599 prepare to set back to Carnforth East Junction with the 12.28am Heysham Moss — Carnforth freight (T84) of May 25 1964.

Below: The stone crushing plant at Silverdale provides a backdrop to Stanier 8F 2-8-0 No. 48055 as it storms towards Carnforth with the 1.25pm freight from Workington (9L92) on May 21 1963.

Right: Borwick station, on the Carnforth-Wennington line on May 25 1964. Here we see 'Black 5' 4-6-0 No. 44893 passing the overgrown platforms with the 10.35 Carnforth-Leeds express, comprised entirely of LMS stock. Borwick closed on September 12 1960 and is now a private residence.

Below 'Crab' 2-6-0 No. 42812 begins the long climb to Clapham at Wennington Junction on September 20 1963 with the 2.50pm Heysham Harbour-Stourton fully-fitted freight. Wennington Junction was a busy location where trains divided for Carnforth and Lancaster and Morecambe. Also visible are the down running loop and refuge siding, now lifted.

EAST TO HELLIFIELD

Another 'Crab' 2-6-0, No. 42798, forges through the once-elegant station at Hellifield with the 2.50pm Heysham Harbour-Stourton fitted freight of September 14 1961. The engine shed coaling stage is visible in the background.

CARNFORTH-CARLISLE

MAIN LINE & BRANCHES

Above: Yealand Conyers, situated between Carnforth and Burton & Holme on the West Coast Main Line, June 16 1963. English Electric Type 4 No. D 377 starts the long haul to Grayrigg with the 11.15am Birmingham - Glasgow (1S61).

Right: The double-track picturesque Windermere branch was heavily used in the summer months, but surprisingly it never seemed to attract many photographers. Riddles 4MT 4-6-0 No. 75060 attacks the fearsome 1 in 80 gradient from Kendal to Oxenholme with the 3.15pm Windermere - Liverpool Exchange of June 25 1964.

Above: Stanier Class 8P No. **46248** *City of Leeds* leaves Oxenholme and gets to grips with Grayrigg bank, hauling the 11.15pm Birmingham-Glasgow on October 4 1961. The Windermere branch slopes away to the right, from the platforms.

Below: The glorious scenery of the Lune Gorge before the intrusion of the M6. 'Austerity' 2-8-0s Nos. 90366 and 90328 rumble towards Dillicar with the 8am Fazakerley-Southwaite prefabricated track train of May 4 1963.

Above: 'EE' Type 4 No. D273 sprints over the Dillicar water troughs in the snow-covered Lune Gorge with the 10.5am Glasgow - Birmingham of November 18 1962. The 13-coach train is a mixture of LMS and BR Mk. 1 stock.

Right: A rainy evening at Tebay as 'Black 5' No. 45021 digs in with the 10.55am Oxley - Carlisle fitted freight of October 5 1963. There are four miles of 1 in 75 climb ahead and judging by the leaking steam, the 4-6-0 is far from its best.

This was the sort of picture that made all the failures worthwhile. Due to a derailment at Stainforth Sidings, on the Settle-Carlisle line on May 9 1963, all Midland line services were diverted via Shap, Low Gill and Clapham. Here we see the fireman on 'Black 5' No. 45313 enjoying the ride downgrade towards Tebay with the diverted 2.50pm Long Meg-Widnes, while up the hill towards Shap Wells comes No. 45329 with the 1.25pm Crewe-Carlisle fitted freight.

Running under clear LNWR lower quadrant signals at Thrimby Grange on May 9 1963 is an English Electric Type 4 No. D 384 with the 10.5am Glasgow-Birmingham (1M24).

Left: With the summit in sight, grubby 'Austerity' 2-8-0 No. 90157 steams steadily uphill at Shap Wells with the 'Tebay ballast' assisted at the rear by one of Tebay's 2-6-4Ts, No. 42414, on June 16 1962, a beautiful clear day.

Right: With the tender tank topped up, Stanier 'Black 5' 4-6-0 No. 45094 gets away from Penrith on May 8 1963 with the 2.4pm Carlisle - Ravenhead Junction freight. A 'water stop' at Penrith for southbound trains was frequently a subterfuge for a 'blow-up'!

Above: A classic country station scene in the Lake District which is now no more. The Station Master closes the doors prior to departure of the 1.31pm Penrith-Workington DMU of June 9 1962. The Keswick-Workington section closed on April 18 1966 and the truncated Penrith-Keswick section followed it into oblivion on March 6 1972. Even the 'Yellow Diamond' DMU class is now extinct.

A busy spell at Carlisle Kingmoor MPD (12A) on September 26 1964. Stabled locomotives include Nos. 73079, 72005 *Clan Macgregor*, 61397, 61244 *Strang Steel* and 45082.

One of the centre roads at Carlisle Citadel is host to 'Jubilee' 4-6-0 No. 45697 *Achilles* and Riddles 'Clan' No. 72008 *Clan Macleod*. The 'Jubilee' was waiting to take over the 12.40pm Gourock-Leicester, London Road, while the 'Pacific' was ready to work the 4.40pm Carlisle-Hellifield. The date was August 7 1965.

MIXED TRAFFIC

Above: The Carlisle SLS/MLS railtour awaits the rightaway from Langholm, to Carlisle behind preserved North British Railway 'Glen' 4-4-0 No. 256 *Glen Douglas*, April 6 1963. This railtour also visited Carlisle 'new' yard at Kingmoor, prior to its opening.

Right: A sunny evening at the trackside near the Express Dairy, Appleby, on May 9 1963. Stanier 5MT 4-6-0 No. 45126 hurries through Appleby West with the 11.55am Brewery - Carlisle mixed freight.

Above: An idyllic image of the country railway, on the North Eastern line between Kirkby Stephen and Penrith. Ivatt 4MT 2-6-0 No. 43023 approaches Appleby East with the 2.40pm Warcop-Carlisle Yard freight of May 3 1963. Scenes like this were typical victims of the Beeching axe.

Centre, left: Industrial steam abounded but was rarely photographed, in comparison with BR steam. This shed grouping at Walkden Colliery on September 17 1964 depicts three Hunslet 'Austerity' 0-6-0STs, one of which is fitted with a Giesl exhaust ejector. A fourth saddletank is just visible under cover beyond the coal wagons on the left.

Below, left: Also at Walkden on the same day: North Staffordshire 0-6-2T No. 2 (built 1922) which was still in traffic at this time. This loco was withdrawn by the LMS in 1937 as No. 2271 and sold to Walkden Collieries, where it was named *Princess*, and continued in service until 1966. The NSR livery was applied for an exhibition in 1958. No. 2 was stored at Shugborough Hall, Staffordshire from 1966 until early 1984, when it was moved to the Mining Museum at Chatterley Whitfield, for static display.

YORK

Approaching Holgate Road bridge on August 7 1961 is Riddles 9F 2-10-0 No. 92116 with a day excursion to Scarborough. The train includes Thompson, Gresley and Stanier stock.

Running neck and neck towards York station at Holgate Road on August 7 1961 are Thompson B1 4-6-0 No. 61023 *Hirola* and Stanier 'Black 5' No. 45268, which is also working a day excursion to Scarborough.

Above: Near-perfect photographic conditions on the south side of Holgate Road bridge, near York station, on August 7 1961. Gresley V2 2-6-2 No. 60961, of York shed, leaves with an up express for King's Cross.

Left: Two-tone green liveried Class 55 'Deltic' No. D 9007 *Pinza* heads south through York with the up 'Flying Scotsman' of August 7 1961. The picture pre-dates the day of the overall yellow warning panel and the locomotive was in immaculate condition.

Above: With the regulator closed and steam roaring from the safety valves, Stanier 5MT No. 45445 drifts towards York, at Holgate Road bridge, en-route to Scarborough on August 7 1961 with a Holiday Express from Barrow-in-Furness, as the enormous headboard proudly proclaims. I wonder what they thought in Scarborough!

Above: The jet of steam under the centre driving wheels shows the sanders are in action on LNER A4 Pacific No. 60034 *Lord Faringdon*, which is at the head of a Newcastle-King's Cross express at York on August 7 1961. The loco was allocated to King's Cross — better known as 'Top Shed'.

Right: Despite the fact that it was taken away from my 'home' patch, this picture near Holgate Bridge remains one of my favourites. In beautiful conditions, Thompson B1 4-6-0 No. 61053 makes a vigorous exit from York with a semi-fast to Sheffield, August 7 1961.

Above: A rare catch for me at the Holgate Road ticket platforms on August 7 1961: LNER B16 4-6-0 No. 61455, in charge of a 12-coach excursion including 11 LMS coaches. Note the condemned Gresley stock in the background.

Right: In their last days the A4s were transferred to the Glasgow - Aberdeen services and I spent a happy weekend photographing them on these duties. Here is No. 60004 *William Whitelaw* at Perth MPD (63A), being prepared to work the 5.10pm Perth-Carstairs of May 9 1965.

ON SHED

Left: Immingham B1 4-6-0 No. 61168 prepares to take coal at Sheffield Darnall shed, (41A) April 8 1962.

Above: A classic image of the working railway at Sheffield Darnall on April 8 1962. Work-stained Thompson B1 4-6-0 No. 61282 is stabled in front of Gresley V2 2-6-2 No. 60956. Power for the B1's electric lights was provided by the steam driven generator seen on the running plate, alongside the smokebox.

With its running fox motif still in place on the boiler cladding, No. 60017 *Silver Fox* stands in the cinders at Gateshead shed (52A) on April 24 1960. This was another 'top shed' engine.

SCOTLAND

Right: The Glasgow & South Western station at Ayr was an impressive backdrop for steam photographs. Riddles 3MT 2-6-0 No. 77017 of Hurlford shed (67B) waits to depart with the 6.43pm working to Glasgow of 16 July 1962.

Below: The teatime local to Ballachulish stands under the overall roof at Oban on April 27 1961, with McIntosh '19' class 2P 0-4-4T No. 55124 at its head. This locomotive was the sole survivor of its class, introduced in 1895. This roof is now said to be unsafe and these tracks have been lifted in recent years.

Oban, April 27 1961, and Stanier 'Black 5' 4-6-0 No. 45366 stands ahead of the stop blocks with the early morning arrival from Glasgow Buchanan street.

WALES

Above: This is how I like to remember the GWR. Running under clear signals at Ruabon on August 16 1961 is Collett 5700 class 0-6-0PT No. 3689, bound for Llangollen.

Right: The classic GWR branch line train. Collett 14XX 0-4-2T No. 1432 is paired with an auto-coach at Wrexham Central station on October 11 1960.

Above: Moat Lane Junction — change for Llanidloes, Rhayader, Builth Wells, Brecon and South Wales. No. 7822 *Foxcote Manor* draws into the now extinct station with an up freight on August 15 1961. This station closed on December 31 1962 — just over a year after this photograph was taken — but the 'Manor' lives on in preservation.

Below: The 'Cambrian Coast Express' leaves Moat Lane Junction behind Machynlleth shed's immaculately turned out 'Manor' 4-6-0 No. 7803 *Barcote Manor* on August 15 1961. This train was a through service from Paddington to Aberystwyth and Pwllheli.

Above: With the tender piled high with coal, No. 7803 *Barcote Manor* stands fully prepared at Aberystwyth shed, prior to working the 'Cambrian Coast Express' of August 15 1961. It was not unusual for engines working this train to be turned out in such pristine condition. This building is now the engine shed for the 1ft 11½in gauge Vale of Rheidol Railway 2-6-2Ts.

A busy scene outside Machynlleth shed (89C) on August 14 1961. The down 'Cambrian Coast Express' approaches the platforms behind 'Manor' 4-6-0s Nos. 7816 *Frilsham Manor* and 7811 *Dunley Manor*. The train divided here and Riddles 2-6-2T No. 82006, standing in the down loop with a Stanier BSK, worked the rear portion to Pwllheli.

Above: The original V of R engine shed at Aberystwyth, which was on the banks of the Afon Rheidol, with No. 9 *Prince of Wales* being prepared for duty, August 15 1961. Note the coal on the tank top, for these locos are now oil-burners.

Left: Three Cocks Junction on October 10 1962 — just two months before closure. Ivatt 2MT 2-6-0 No. 46503 stands in the station platform with the 12.40pm Hereford-Three Cocks Junction working. This was once a busy junction of lines from Moat Lane Junction, Brecon and Hereford: all three routes closed on December 31 1962.

Home was in the north but I made many trips to the Southern in pursuit of steam, and this photograph was taken during a visit to the Swanage branch. Rebuilt Bulleid 'Merchant Navy' Pacific No. 35021 *New Zealand Line* brakes for its Wareham stop on the 11.30am Weymouth-Waterloo of October 22 1963.

SOUTHERN STEAM

Above: Drummond M7 0-4-4T No. 30107 takes water at Wareham after arriving with the 11.40am from Swanage of October 22 1963. This branch survived until closure on January 3 1972 and it is now the subject of a preservation plan.

Left: One of the few surviving Maunsell S15 4-6-0s, No. 30837, of Feltham shed (70B), leaves Eastleigh yard with an up freight, October 24 1963.

Right: An everyday picture of Southern steam in its last years: 'N' Class 2-6-0 No. 31405 stands in the sun alongside the coaling stage at Eastleigh (71A) on June 10 1965.

Below: With a clear road ahead from Bournemouth Central, a full head of steam and one minute to departure time, the driver of No. 35019 *French Line CGT* tops up the tank while the fireman pulls coal forward onto the shovelling plate. The train is the 10.8am Bournemouth West - Waterloo, October 22 1963.

Left: The signals are off and No. 34025 *Whimple* awaits the guard's right-away with the 10.50am Bournemouth West-York of June 9 1965.

Below: Riddles Class 5 4-6-0 No. 73043 gets away from Bournemouth Central with the 10am Bournemouth West - Liverpool Lime Street of June 10 1965. Rebuilt Bulleid 'West Country' Pacific No. 34024 *Tamar Valley* waits on one of the centre roads with an ECS train.

Crossing the road entrance to Southampton pier on May 3 1961 is LBSC Billinton E4 0-6-2T No. 32556, with a yard-to-yard transfer freight. This class was introduced in 1897.

THE ISLE OF WIGHT

Six months before the end of steam working on the Isle of Wight system. Adams LSWR Class 02 0-4-4T No. 35 *Freshwater* hauls six non-corridor coaches forming the 2.25pm Ryde Pier-Ventnor of June 7 1965. Originally introduced in 1889, the 02s were fitted with Westinghouse brake equipment in 1923.

Left: No. 35 *Freshwater* makes a brisk departure from Ryde St. Johns with the 12.18 Ryde Pier-Cowes of June 7 1965. Another of the IOW's great attractions was the vintage rolling stock, clearly seen in this view.

Below: Within a year of this photograph being taken, this Victorian railway had gone. Here we see 02 No. 16 *Ventnor*, in comparatively clean condition, standing at Ventnor with the 17.42 to Ryde Pier, June 7 1965. The Ventnor - Shanklin route closed on April 4 1966.

EVERCREECH JUNCTION

Begrimed Riddles 4MT 4-6-0 No. 75073 comes to a stand at Evercreech Junction on June 11 1965 with the 3.20pm Bath Green Park–Bournemouth West working, comprised of Bulleid stock.

THE ISLE OF MAN

Above: The Isle of Man Railway is a long standing favourite and I have visited it many times. The line's unique character and appeal are clear in this picture of a three-coach Ramsey branch train arriving at Douglas on August 7 1963, behind 2-4-0T No. 5 *Mona*. The need for extensive track repairs prompted closure of the Ramsey branch in 1968.

Below: This is now a car park! Beyer Peacock 2-4-0T No. 10 *G. H. Wood* (works No. 4662 of 1905) prepares to pilot a Ramsey-Douglas train at St Johns, which also closed in 1968. Probably few of the visitors who park their cars here today realise that the railway ever existed.

Above: A typical IOMR scene of the early 1960s as 2-4-0T No. 11 *Maitland* (works No. 4663 of 1905) prepares to leave Castletown with a Douglas — Port Erin train, June 17 1960. The IOMR lorry was collecting parcels. This section is still open — and little changed today.

The ex-County Donegal Railway Walker Brothers bogie diesel railcars Nos. 19/20 (built 1950/51) leave St Johns, en-route to Kirk Michael, on August 8 1963. These railcars, bought by the IOMR in 1961 are retained in working order today to cover in the event of steam failures.

Above: 2-4-0T No. 6 *Peveril* (built 1875) takes water at Peel on June 17 1960, having worked in from Douglas. The Peel branch, from St Johns, also closed in 1968 when major track renewal became necessary.

Right: Douglas station, June 17 1960. 2-4-0T No. 13 *Kissack* (works No. 5382 of 1910) awaits departure for Ramsey. My father, Arthur Herbert, is standing next to the open door with his copy of the 'Bradshaw' timetable. He never went anywhere without it! The overall station roof has since been dismantled.

BROMSGROVE

Above: Bromsgrove, at the foot of the notorious Lickey Incline, on July 14 1962. Coasting off the 1 in 37 gradient with safety valves blowing is Stanier 'Black 5' 4-6-0 No. 44660 with a relief Birmingham New Street-Bournemouth West service. Note the pigeon baskets on the up platform.

A combined potential tractive effort of more than 62,000 lbs storms through Bromsgrove station to do battle with the Lickey incline on July 14 1962. Hawksworth 94XX 0-6-0PT No. 8402 and Riddles 9F 2-10-0 No. 92079 were giving vigorous assistance to Riddles 5MT 4-6-0 No. 73003 with 'The Pines Express'. I shall never forget the sound these two locomotives made!

IRELAND

Right: Ireland's 5ft. 3in. gauge system was an irresistible draw for me from 1961 and in 1964 — as the end approached — I was making the crossing about once a month. Unusual machines were always a characteristic of the Irish scene and here we see derelict GNR crane tank No. 31 in the scrap road at Inchicore Works, Dublin, on July 28 1964.

Below: On July 28 1964, GNR class VS 4-4-0 No. 207 *Boyne* is turned at Dublin Amiens Street shed, having arrived with a day excursion from Belfast. No. 207, built in Manchester by Beyer Peacock in 1948, was painted in blue livery and looked magnificent.

Above: The Irish also had their own distinctive approach to the railbus principle, as this converted road vehicle at Inchicore Works illustrates! It is GNR railcar No. 8177 and was photographed on October 22 1961.

Left: More examples of the Irish railbus builders art at Inchicore, also pictured on October 22 1961. The vehicle was operated by the CIE — though how successfully is not recorded! The flat wagon behind the railbus is carrying a narrow gauge railcar cab — it is not a double-deck railbus prototype as might first appear!

Right: Northern Counties Committee (NCC) Class WT 2-6-4T No. 53 stands in the station yard at Warrenpoint on August 2 1964 with the empty stock of a day excursion from Belfast Great Victoria Street, which is now closed. These engines were Derby built — and it shows. The locos were shipped in sections to Northern Ireland, via Heysham.

Below: Portadown MPD, on the Belfast-Dublin line, on August 9 1964. The loco in the foreground is class 'U' 4-4-0 No. 67 *Louth*.

Above: This was the sort of picture which enticed me back to Ireland again and again — if only it were the same today! This is Strabane on May 20 1964, with GNR 'S' class 4-4-0 No. 60 *Slieve Donard* on station pilot duty. The remains of the County Donegal Joint Railway station is visible in the background.

Left: An almost timeless scene at Dungannon, on the GNR main line from Belfast to Londonderry on July 18 1963. GNR 'S' class 4-4-0 No. 170 *Errigal* stands alongside a magnificent water column and signal with the 3pm Belfast Great Victoria Street - Londonderry Foyle Road service.

Above: NCC Class 'W' 2-6-0 No. 91 *The Bush* stands in the sun outside the GNR loco shed at Londonderry on March 21 1964. Note the apparatus on the cab side for catching tablets used on single line sections. These engines were built between 1933 and 1942 by the LMS at Derby.

Right: Shunting in the GNR Londonderry goods yard on July 18 1963 is GNR Class 'SG2' 0-6-0 No. 52, one of a class built between 1913 and 1924 by Clifford. The tender has a distinct LMS family resemblance.

Left: Inside Belfast Transport Museum. The loco is NCC Class 'U2' 4-4-0 No. 74 *Dunluce Castle*, built by the North British Locomotive Company, at Glasgow, in 1924. Withdrawn from service in 1961, the 4-4-0 was donated by the Ulster Transport Authority to the Museum, where it is still on show today.

Below: Belfast Adelaide MPD. Standing amongst the piles of ashes on August 3 1964 are NCC Class 'W' 2-6-0 No. 91 *The Bush* and GNR Class 'SG3' 0-6-0 No. 47. Pictures like this epitomise the appeal of Irish steam.

SPAIN
& ITALY

Above: I also travelled to Europe for the sole purpose of photographing steam, and Spain's 5ft. 6in. gauge locomotives were an impressive and distinctive breed. On the right, 4-8-2 No. 241F2110 tops up with sand at Miranda de Ebro on September 27 1967, alongside 4-8-4 No. 242-2008. Both locomotives are fitted with standard RENFE electric headlights.

Right: On January 21 1967, 0-6-0T No. 851.107 shunts vans on the dock at Syracuse, Southern Sicily, in front of quayside tenements. This was an Italian State Railways locomotive.

Sunday afternoon at Madrid Delicias roundhouse, September 30 1967. Stabled on shed are (left to right): 2-8-2 No. 141F2330; 4-8-0 No. 240F2610; 4-8-0 No. 240F2561 and 4-8-0 No. 240F2599. The corrugated roofed trolley was used by shed fitters for moving their welding equipment about!

'The Fleche D'Or' — the French connecting service of 'The Golden Arrow' — crosses the River Liane at Boulogne on May 18 1965 behind 'Pacific' No. 231E17. This train was booked to leave Calais at 2.37pm, bound for Paris Nord.

FRANCE & GERMANY

Below: A majestic sight at Boulogne, also on May 18 1965, as 'Liberator' 2-8-2s Nos. 141R348 and 141R311 run light-engines to the shed.

Left: Koblenz, Deutches Bundesbahn, September 29 1965. The guard of the 2.36pm to Paris East gives details of the train formation to the driver of '01' Pacific No. 01.059. With his green uniform, red sash and braided cap, the guard cut an impressive figure.

Below: Class 50 DB 2-10-0 No. 50.1919 stands on the turntable in the autumn sunshine at Munich MPD, September 25 1965. The locomotive had been towed out of the roundhouse courtesy of the shed staff, just for us to photograph it. The staff were pleasant and helpful and all the locos were shunted out one by one, for our cameras.

THE ROMNEY, HYTHE & DYMCHURCH RAILWAY

Above: The miniature main line of the RHDR remains a firm favourite and I have spent many happy hours at its tracksides. On May 21 1965 Yorkshire Engine Co. 'Pacific' No. 9 *Winston Churchill* (built 1931) is ready to depart from New Romney with a train for Hythe. Note the bell behind the chimney, which adds the finishing touch to the 'Pacific's' American outline.

Right: The elegant and beautifully proportioned lines of Davey Paxman 4-6-2 No. 7 *Typhoon* (built 1926) are evident in this low viewpoint picture at Hythe, May 21 1965.

Left: Davey Paxman 2-8-2 No. 1 *Green Goddess* (built 1925) drifts through Woodland near New Romney with the first train of the day on May 22 1965.

Below: There's not a speck of dirt or a wisp of stray steam to be seen from No. 7 *Typhoon*, pictured waiting to depart from Hythe with 'The Marshlander' of May 21 1965. The locomotive was immaculate and a real credit to its driver and the Railway. This was steam at its best: well cared-for and performing to perfection — it was in stark contrast to the sorry condition of the greater part of BR's surviving steam fleet at this time.

The end of steam on the Southern Region. Rebuilt Bulleid 'Merchant Navy' Pacific No. **35023** *Holland Afrika Line* stands at Weymouth with the 8.30am Waterloo-Weymouth of Saturday July 8 1967. This was the last full day of steam on the Southern and after this only the London Midland Region kept steam engines at work; by August 1968 they too had gone. I was in Traffic Control at this time and operationally steam had become a nightmare. Failures, shortages of steam and late running habitually resulted from the poor state of the engines and as a Controller I couldn't help sighing with relief when the last fires had been dropped. However, as a lover of steam I was as saddened as everyone else. The Working Railway would never be quite the same, ever again.

Part 2

Awaiting a clear road south from Dent, on the Midland Railway's spectacular Settle-Carlisle line over the fells, is class 45 diesel-electric No. D44, coupled to the 10.5am Carlisle-Stourton freight on March 12 1963. Note the six-wheeled milk tank, and the steps cut into D44's body panels adjacent to the cab door - these gave access to the filler cap on the locomotive roof through which the steam train heating boiler reservoir could be replenished (see also page 109). Today the lonely signal box, refuge sidings, crossover and cattle dock have gone, leaving just the double track up and down lines, themselves once under threat of closure.

PRESTON

Right: Preston station at 2.50pm on March 19 1963 as English Electric Type 4 No. D 214 *Antonia* is uncoupled from the 9am Perth-Euston, prior to running over the scissors crossover and attaching the portion which left Workington at 10.53am, after which the Type 4 will take the whole train on south. Both north and south main platforms at Preston were equipped with scissors crossovers to facilitate this kind of remarshalling, which is less common today.

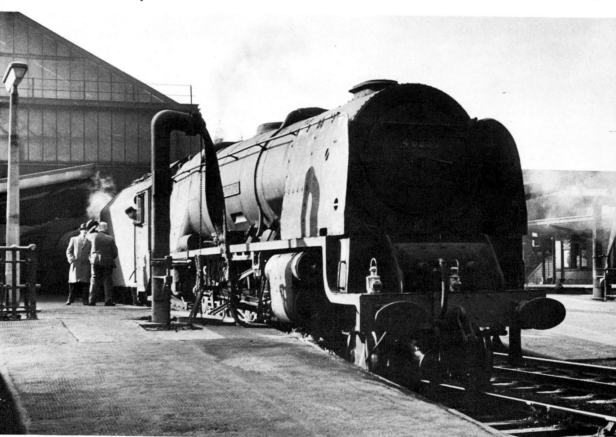

Stanier's mighty 'Princess Coronation' class 8P 'Pacifics', a familiar sight on the West Coast Main Line for many years, were nearing the end of their working lives when this picture was taken on March 22 1963. No. 46230 *Duchess of Buccleuch* awaits a clear road north from Preston, at the head of the 9.53pm Willesden-Carlisle parcels. Originally a crimson-liveried non-streamlined engine built in 1938, No. 46230 also carried the experimental BR blue livery for express engines in May 1948. It was withdrawn from service in lined Brunswick green livery in November 1963 and was cut up for scrap before the end of the year at Crewe Works.

Above: No. 46240 *City of Coventry* remarshals the 'Horse & Carriage' (the 8.15am Carlisle-Crewe parcels) at Preston June 8 1964.

Left: Leaving the southern end of Preston station on June 22 1963 is Stanier '8P' 4–6–2 No. 46225 *Duchess of Gloucester* with a special Glasgow-Euston working (1X76), which ran non-stop through Preston, under the scrutiny of a band of young trainspotters positioned in the entrance to the former LMS Park Hotel, high on the left of the picture. 46225 was scrapped in September 1964 after running nearly 1¾ million miles in revenue-earning service since entering traffic in May 1938.

Taking the old 'up through' road at Preston on March 23 1963 is Stanier '5MT' 4–6–0 No. 45191, at the head of the 8.54am Carnforth-Ince Moss freight. At this time I was a Traffic Controller at Preston. This area is now the concrete apron for Preston's parcels concentration depot: the up and down through roads were completely removed and the track adjacent to the platform was severed and the centre section removed to form two sidings.

Riddles class 7P 'Britannia' 4–6–2 No. 70052 *Firth of Tay*, then allocated to Crewe North Shed (5A), eases away from the platform at Preston on February 26 1963 with the 11.30am Birmingham-Glasgow train. This 'Pacific,' built at Crewe Works in August 1954, was cut up and weighed in for scrap at Campbell's yard, Airdrie in November 1967 after being taken out of traffic in April of the same year. It was just 12 years and 8 months old at withdrawal.

Left: Stanier 'Black 5' 4–6–0 No. 44986 stands in the former No. 3 platform at Preston station on March 22 1963, awaiting the rightaway with the 2.54pm Preston-Barrow service. The 4–6–0 is paired with the 'self weighing' tender used by engineers to assess coal consumption in performance tests.

Below: Stanier '8P' No. 46251 *City of Nottingham* gets to grips with the 'Horse and Carriage' — the 8.15am Carlisle-Crewe parcels (3K16) of September 20 1963. This train was so-called as in its early days it regularly carried horses and carriages, and the nickname persisted at least until the end of BR steam working in 1968.

NORTH TO LANCASTER

Right: The 2.40pm Pilling-Preston North Union goods — known locally as 'The Pilling Pig' — leaves Pilling on March 23 1962 with No. 45388. The Garstang & Knott End Railway, closed to passengers on March 31 1930 but which remained open for freight traffic, was shortened to Pilling prior to complete closure in 1965.

Above: Disturbing the peace south of Lancaster on September 1 1962 is Stanier '8P' No. 46256 *Sir Wiliam A Stanier FRS*, in charge of the 10.15am Glasgow-Euston (1M25). The gradient here is 1 in 98 — a taxing climb for any locomotive, whether or not it stopped at Lancaster.

Right: unique Riddles 'Pacific' No. 71000 *Duke of Gloucester* was an infrequent visitor to Lancaster: the engine is seen here at the south end of Castle station's platform 4 with the 'Horse and Carriage,' the 8.15am Carlisle-Crewe parcels (3K16) on August 29 1961. This locomotive is now on the Great Central Railway.

Above: The clear exhaust and surplus steam billowing from one of the safety valves indicates that Riddles 'Britannia' 4–6–2 No. 70045 *Lord Rowallan* is working well on the southbound climb from Lancaster Castle station, with the 10.35am Glasgow-Blackpool (1M21) of June 16 1961. Note the Travelling Post Office mail bag pick-up apparatus mounted on the chequered base adjacent to the down main line, near the telegraph pole, and the articulated LMS set comprising the second and third vehicles of the train.

Left: With the regulator closed and steam roaring from its Ross 'pop' safety valves, rebuilt 'Royal Scot' 4–6–0 No. 46162 *Queen's Westminster Rifleman* rolls downgrade towards Lancaster Castle station at the head of the 1.30pm Manchester-Glasgow of July 1 1962.

Leaving Lancaster Castle's platform 5 on August 31 1961 is Crewe North shed's rebuilt 'Royal Scot' 4–6–0 No. 46110 *Grenadier Guardsman*, at the head of the 12.50pm Barrow-Euston. The cattle dock on the right once handled extensive livestock traffic.

A very rare photograph indeed! North British-built diesel-hydraulic 'Warship' No. D854 *Tiger*, in gleaming ex-works condition, hurries through the up fast road at Lancaster Castle station en-route from Glasgow to Swindon for commissioning into traffic, September 14 1961. *Tiger* might have heralded the new era of modern traction — but it still carried an ancient oil-headlamp! The locomotive had a relatively short life: it was withdrawn in October 1971 and was dismantled at Swindon Works in May 1972.

Left: The Modernisation Plan in action: the 'fireman' (the designation 'second man' had yet to be adopted) of 'Peak' diesel-electric No. D6 *Whernside* watches water spurt from a very leaky leather 'bag' as he replenishes the train heating boiler whilst working the 8.40am Carlisle-Euston of October 30 1961. Note the cast-iron braziers, used to prevent the water columns freezing during the winter.

Above: A southbound departure from Castle station, as seen from Lancaster No. 2 signalbox. Unrebuilt 'Patriot' 4–6–0 No. 45533 *Lord Rathmore* barks up the grade with the 2.30pm Morecambe-Crewe (W266) of March 25 1961. The six coach train is comprised of a standard Mk 1 BG, two Stanier vehicles, two Great Western vehicles and a final Stanier coach. None of the 'Patriots' survived into preservation: No. 45533 was withdrawn in September 1962, stored at Edge Hill shed (8A) Liverpool and finally cut up for scrap at Crewe Works in October 1962. The up yard at Lancaster has since been completely erased.

Left: This was the view from the south end of Lancaster No. 3 signalbox on August 22 1961 as '8P' No. 46228 *Duchess of Rutland* rolls into platform 3 with the 9.20am Crewe-Perth (1S53).

Stanier 'Princess Royal' 4–6–2 No. 46209 *Princess Beatrice* — an uncommon visitor — sprints through the up fast line road at Lancaster Castle with the 10.15am Glasgow-Euston (1M25) of August 5 1961.

An impressive view from the base of Lancaster No. 4 signal box on June 20 1964 as rebuilt 'Royal Scot' 4–6–0 No. 46166 *London Rifle Brigade* gets away from Castle station's No. 3 platform with the 1.30pm Manchester Victoria-Glasgow service. A Metro-Vick Co-Bo diesel is just visible on the right, awaiting a clear road from the No. 1 bay platform with a train for Barrow. At this time No. 46166 had less than four months life ahead: it was withdrawn in October 1964 and by the year-end it had been broken up for scrap by the West of Scotland Shipbreaking Company, at Troon.

In clear afternoon sunlight, Crew North Shed's Stanier three-cylinder 'Jubilee' 4–6–0 No. 45689 *Ajax* climbs past Lancaster No. 3 signal box, hauling the 10.53am Workington-Preston of February 13 1962. The pre-Grouping pattern signalbox was numbered in accordance of LNWR west coast practice of numbering a station's signal boxes from the south.

Right: With steam wheezing from its piston rod and valve spindle glands, Springs Branch-based LNWR 'Super D' 0–8–0 No. 49447 beats it's distinctive way south, opposite Lancaster No. 4 signal box, with the 10.25am Carnforth-Warrington goods of June 11 1962. The veteran carriage in the background had survived in service as a S&T engineers tool van.

Shaking the ground as it sweeps round the curving northern approach to Lancaster Castle station is 'Princess Coronation' No. 46229 *Duchess of Hamilton*, in complete mastery of a relief working from Glasgow to Kensington Olympia (1X79) on April 5 1963. The '8P', now maintained in operating condition to main line standards by the National Railway Museum, York, is passing Lancaster No. 4 signal box and the junction for the Glasson Dock branch.

Top: The southern end of Lancaster No. 4 box was a superb vantage post, and one of my favourite photographic locations, which on March 22 1963 featured Stanier 'Jubilee' 4–6–0 No. 45704 *Leviathan*, paired with a narrow Fowler tender, leaving No. 3 platform with the 2.54pm Preston-Barrow (1L21) comprised of just three vehicles, of which the centre coach is of Fowler design. In bay platform No. 2, a Stanier 2–6–4T is waiting to depart bunker-first with a local service for Bare Lane and Morecambe. Note that the Glasson dock branch, diverging to the right, was accessible from the down slow (platform 3) as well as both bay platforms (Nos. 1 and 2).

Above: Running cautiously down the sharply curved and checkrailed gradient from Lancaster Castle to Green Ayre on March 24 1963 is English Electric Type 4 (later class 40) No. D 325 at the head of 1L98 — the 10.25pm Willesden-Carlisle parcels. This picture was taken whilst 'Carlisle bridge' carrying the West Coast Main Line over the River Lune at Lancaster, was being rebuilt, with the consequent diversion of Anglo-Scottish services via Green Ayre, Morecambe Promenade and Bare Lane.

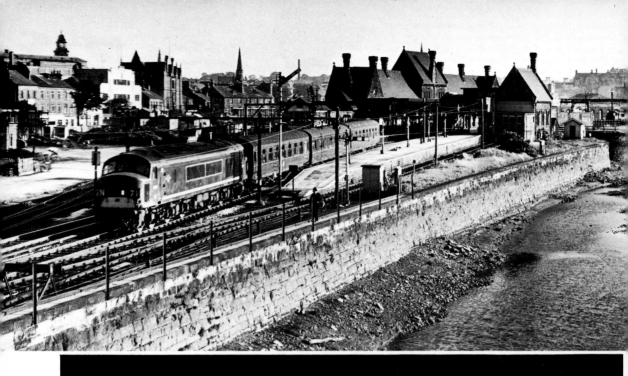

THE 'LITTLE NORTH WESTERN'

Above: Lancaster Green Ayre station, viewed from Skerton Bridge, on June 26 1963, as diesel-electric No. D 27 (later designated class 45) departs with three LMS coaches forming the 7.17pm Morecambe-Leeds (2N71). The Lancaster Green Ayre-Wennington Junction link closed on January 3 1966 and this site has since been redeveloped as a riverside park. Standing in the same spot today, you'd never know the railway had ever been here.

Right, above: This is now part of Lancaster's Sainsbury's supermarket development! However, on August 22 1961 this was Lancaster Green Ayre shed, with Ivatt '4' 2–6–0 No. 43112 and rebuilt 'Royal Scot' No. 46102 *Black Watch*, of Polmadie shed, in residence.

Right, below: In Lancaster Green Ayre shed yard, Ivatt '4' 2–6–0 No. 43130, of Leeds Holbeck shed, is prepared for a trip back to Yorkshire in the late evening of June 7 1963. A 'Jinty' 0–6–0T stands alongside.

Approaching Heysham Moss from Morecambe on August 31 1962 is Horwich 'Crab' 2–6–0 No. 42776 with a train of empty fuel tanks from the Midland Division. This double track link survived in 1986, but with little traffic. The catenary was used by the Lancaster-Morecambe-Heysham electric passenger services.

Metro-Vick Co-Bo diesel No D 5711 leads a rake of Stanier coaches forming the diverted 10.45am Barrow-Preston up the steeply graded curving link between Lancaster Green Ayre and Lancaster Castle stations on March 24 1963. Greyhound bridge, seen in the background carrying the Green Ayre-Morecambe line across the River Lune was retained following closure of this line on January 3 1966, and now carries the northbound carriageway of the A6 trunk road out of Lancaster.

Leaving Scale Hall station, bound for Morecambe on January 24 1964, is EMU No. M28220M, forming the 12.10pm from Lancaster Castle. The Lancaster-Morecambe-Heysham line had been electrified by the Midland Railway in 1908 but by 1953 the original units were in utterly ramshackle condition: but for the war they would probably have been scrapped years before. Thus in 1951 the MR cars were replaced by a steam auto-service worked by 0–4–4Ts, whilst the overhead supply was converted to 25 kilovolt operation. The 'new' units, built in 1914 for the Willesden-Earls Court service, were transferred to Lancaster, painted green and entered service in their new role on August 17 1953. They were withdrawn with closure of the line on January 3 1966.

Thompson 'B1' 4–6–0 No. 61173 approaches Scale Hall, from Heysham, with the 2.50pm Heysham Harbour-Stourton fitted freight of September 1 1964. At this time this line ran through open fields: today a housing development occupies the far side of the line whilst behind me nowadays is Lancaster's Asda superstore and car park. The appearance of a 'B1' on this turn was very rare — it was normally a Green Ayre duty.

Above: The clock tower alongside Caton Road, Lancaster, survived in 1986 as a recognisable landmark, but this tidy piece of railway disappeared from the network on January 3 1966. With a 24L (Carnforth) shedplate on its smokebox door, Stanier 2–6–4T No. 42571 drifts past Ladies Walk Sidings, Lancaster, towards Green Ayre Station with the 1.54pm Leeds-Morecambe of June 23 1962. Once again, the train is a fascinating mixture of stock including non-corridor BR Standard, Gresley, Thompson and Fowler types!

Left: Crossing the Lune at Caton is diesel-electric Sulzer Type 2 No. D 5178, with the 9.33am Morecambe-Leeds (2N71) of June 3 1963. The bridge survives today, used only by hikers and wildlife.

Above: This section of railway is now a footpath. On June 3 1963 BR diesel-electric No. D 21 approaches Caton on the 'Little North Western' route between Wennington Junction and Lancaster with a Leeds-Morecambe day excursion. Built by BR at Derby Works and introduced in March 1961, D 21 was renumbered 45 026 under the TOPS system and was still in traffic in early 1986.

Right: Halton, two miles east of Lancaster Green Ayre station, on July 24 1963 with Horwich 'Crab' 2–6–0 No. 42888 drifting past with the 3.30pm Stourton-Heysham freight. No. 42888 was taken out of traffic in February 1964 and subsequently scrapped by the Central Wagon Company, at Wigan.

Top: A pleasing image of the country railway at Wennington, with '5MT' No. 44889 leading the 8.50am Bradford-Morecambe (2M73) away from the junction with the Carnforth line, bound for Lancaster, on June 3 1963.

Above: Running briskly towards Lancaster, at Halton, is Fowler 2–6–4T No. 42359, a Carnforth engine, with the 1.53pm service from Leeds to Morecambe, March 23 1963.

Left: Hellifield shed on March 12 1963, with snowplough-fitted Fowler 0–6–0s Nos. 44276 and 44149 awaiting their next turn of line clearance duty.

The gradient from Bare Lane station to the West Coast Main Line at Morecambe South Junction was at 1 in 75, and trains sometimes stalled before reaching the main line metals. On this occasion however, Fowler 2–6–4T No. 42314 was master of its task with a train of vans forming the 3.10pm Heysham Harbour-Farington freight of October 2 1961.

Photographed from the top of Morecambe South Junction's up Morecambe branch home signal, rebuilt 'Royal Scot' No. 46129 *The Scottish Horse* clatters over the diamond crossing adjacent to the LNWR signalbox with the 11.20am Euston-Workington (1L28) of June 3 1961. The junction opened in May 1888, boat trains for Heysham diverging from the WCML at this point until the daily Heysham-Belfast sailings ended in April 1975. The signalbox disappeared with the commissioning of Preston power box in January 1973.

Left: On April 17 1960 Stanier '5MT' No. 44682 runs wrong line towards Lancaster, with the 8.20am Workington-Euston Sundays-only service. Relaying of the main line over a one-mile section, about ½ mile from Morecambe South Junction, was being done by traditional manual methods, rather than by the use of prefabricated panels.

Below: My father Arthur Herbert, then Station Master at Bare Lane, stands back as Fairburn 2–6–4T No. 42136 comes off the single line section from Hest Bank at Bare Lane and crosses onto the down line to Morecambe with 'The Lake Windermere Cruise,' (the 4.55pm Lakeside-Morecambe) of June 20 1962. This was an officially named train — note the carriage nameboards above the windows.

The fireman of Stanier 'Jubilee' 4–6–0 No. 45703 *Thunderer* leans out at Bare Lane to collect the tablet for the single line section to the West Coast Main Line at Hest Bank, on September 28 1964. The '5XP' was working the 2.38pm Morecambe-Glasgow (1X34) — a return Glasgow 'long weekend' special.

The same location at Bare Lane, viewed from the down platform, on March 3 1963 as English Electric Type 4 diesel-electric No. D 291 passes with the 9.35am Manchester Victoria-Glasgow service, diverted at Lancaster Castle via Green Ayre, Morecambe, Bare Lane and Hest Bank during the rebuilding of Carlisle Bridge over the Lune at Lancaster. Waiting by the gates is green and cream liveried Morecambe & Heysham bus No. 68, built by AEC Regent in 1950.

Above: 'Patriot' 4–6–0s, especially in original condition, were always a favourite subject: this is un-named No. 45510, of Carlisle Upperby shed (12B), passing Bare Lane in charge of the 11.36am banana special from Garston Dock to Heysham Harbour, April 17 1961. This train was comprised of insulated containers, but when ordinary vehicles were used on this traffic, Control had to provide steam-heat fitted locomotives to ensure that the fruit was kept in good condition during transit.

Left: Attacking the 1 in 75 climb from Bare Lane to the WCML at Morecambe South Junction on June 3 1961 is very grubby Riddles 'Britannia' 4–6–2 No. 70048 *The Territorial Army 1908–58*, hauling a return day excursion to Morecambe, from Birmingham (W645). This picture once again illustrates the marvellous variety of rolling stock to be seen at this time: the nine coach train includes stock of Stanier, Fowler and Great Western origin. The track diverging in the foreground is the single line spur to Hest Bank.

Above: Approaching Bare Lane from Hest Bank on March 3 1963 is English Electric Type 4 No. D 313, at the head of the 10.5am Glasgow-Birmingham (1M24), diverted during the rebuilding of Carlisle Bridge at Lancaster. No. D 313 became 40 113 under the TOPS system, and was withdrawn from service after 21 years in traffic in October 1981, although it was not dismantled for scrap at Swindon works until January 1984. The class is now extinct from capital stock.

Right: On summer Saturdays, the spectacle of engines coupled in threes (sometimes more) running through Bare Lane, bound for Carnforth shed for servicing, was a common sight. In one of these movements, on July 21 1960, we see Stanier '5MTs' Nos. 45323, 45158 *Glasgow Yeomanry* and an unidentified Stanier 2–6–4T running in reverse through Bare Lane station.

Their flat-fronted design and Co-Bo wheel arrangement gave these Metro-Vick locomotives a very unusual appearance. Out in the fields, Co-Bo No. D 5702, of Workington Shed, approaches Hest Bank on the single track spur from Bare Lane, with the 6.50pm Heysham Moss-Corkickle fuel oil tank train. Delivered to the LMR in 1958–9, the class of 20 locomotives were powered by Crossley two-stroke diesel engines, but reliability was poor and after a relatively short life the class was scrapped. This picture was taken on June 10 1964.

Top: Heavy trains heading for the WCML at Morecambe South Junction were held at Bare Lane's inner home signal until the road was clear, this practice giving the enginemen their best chance at having a good run at the taxing 1 in 75 curving climb to the junction. With safety valves roaring and light grey smoke indicating a well burnt-through fire, the fireman is ready for the task ahead in the cab of Stanier '8P' 4–6–2 No. 46250 *City of Lichfield*, waiting at the signal with the 4.30pm Heysham Harbour-Crewe parcels (3K17) of June 29 1963. The level crossing is immediately behind me at this point.

Above: Metro-Vick Co-Bo No. D 5719 passes Bare Lane's outer home signal, on the Hest Bank spur, with the ten-vehicle 10.54am Barrow-Preston of March 3 1963, diverted during the bridge work at Lancaster. The WCML formation is visible in the background.

Left: In the early evening of Sunday August 5 1961 at Bare Lane, Stanier '5XP' 4–6–0 No. 45706 *Express* has a clear road to Morecambe South Junction with the 7.10pm Morecambe-Manchester Victoria. The first four coaches are non-corridor vechicles known locally as 'wides.' Diverging beneath the 'Jubilee's' tender is Bare Lane's solitary siding, which led to the station's coal yard.

Below: Balloon Sidings, Morecambe (Bare Lane station house is visible in the distance on the right) were used for stabling the empty stock from trains working into Euston Road station. On April 25 1962 '8P' No. 46244 *King George VI*, of Kingmoor shed (12A), is stabling the empty stock of a working from Birmingham New Street, after which the 'Pacific' would run light-engine tender first, to Carnforth shed for servicing.

Above: The TSS *Duke of Lancaster* at the north quay, Heysham, on March 16 1965, awaiting its next sailing to Belfast. This service ended in April 1975, after which the Heysham-Morecambe rail link closed to passengers, on October 8 1975. The *Duke of Lancaster* was built for BR in 1956 by Harland & Wolff, of Belfast, and tipped the scales at nearly 4,800 tons. In 1967 the ship was converted to function as a stern-loading car ferry, in which form it performed the last Belfast-Heysham sailing of April 6 1975. The 'Duke' escaped the breaker and was berthed at its present home, Deeside, following withdrawal. Heysham has been rejuvenated in recent years as it is now the base for the Isle of Man Steam Packet Company's sailings to the Isle of Man, but while freight rail services continue to serve Heysham Moss, there is no passenger link to Morecambe and Lancaster.

This was the scene at Heysham Harbour Junction on May 23 1964 as Ivatt 2MT 2-6-0 No. 46441 (now preserved at Steamtown, Carnforth), departs tender-first with the Railway Correspondence & Travel Society's Ribble-Lune railtour. Note the articulated set next to the engine, and the overhead supply for the Lancaster-Morecambe-Heysham electric trains. The signalbox closed with the remodelling of Heysham Harbour station and a replacement provided which was subsequently mothballed.

HEST BANK

Above: On a pleasant, sunny evening at Hest Bank on August 5 1961, Crewe North shed's 'Jubilee' 4–6–0 No. 45723 *Fearless* leads the 6.41pm Preston-Millom past Fairburn 4MT 2–6–4T No. 42135 from Lancaster Green Ayre shed, which is awaiting acceptance onto the WCML with the 7.25pm goods from Morecambe to Carnforth. Behind the '5XP's' tender is a four-wheeled box van, for parcels!

Left: A majestic sight indeed: Stanier 'Princess Coronation' No. 46236 *City of Bradford*, a Carlisle Kingmoor (12A) engine, at full chat south of Hest Bank on November 21 1962 with the 9.30am Glasgow-Liverpool Exchange (1M27). Built in July 1939 as a streamlined locomotive, No. 46236 ran more than 1½ million miles in revenue earning service before being withdrawn in March 1964. Crewe works quickly despatched the 'Pacific' for scrap, in the following month.

I was particularly happy with this study of rebuilt 'Royal Scot' 4-6-0 No. 46160 *Queen Victoria's Rifleman*, a Carlisle Kingmoor (12A) engine, working steadily south near Hest Bank on February 9 1963 with the 10.25am Carlisle-Warrington goods. The heavily loaded telegraph poles at the lineside are of interest for they are increasingly rare today.

Left: A very rare visitor to our patch on August 5 1961 was this locomotive: Stanier 2–6–0 No. 42948 — or 'Lobsters' as the class was known locally — from Crewe South shed (5B). It was approaching Hest Bank with the 10.55am Oxley-Law Junction goods. Sole survivor of this class in preservation is No. 42968, based on the Severn Valley Railway.

Grimy Carlisle Kingmoor-allocated Riddles 'Britannia' 4–6–2 No. 70003 *John Bunyan* crosses from the up main at Hest Bank station, to take the single track link to Bare Lane with the 1.26pm Glasgow-Morecambe of July 25 1964. Like all the 'Standard' types, the 'Britannias' had terribly short lives: *John Bunyan*, built at Crewe Works in March 1951 was withdrawn in March 1967 after just 16 years service. Eight months in store followed at Kingmoor, after which Campbell's at Airdrie converted No. 70003 into slightly more than 140 tons of scrap.

Right: Following the major mishap of May 20 1965, when the 10.10pm Glasgow-Kensington (1V42) was derailed at Hest Bank, steam cranes from Lostock Hall and Carlisle Kingmoor were called to assist in clearance operations. The cranes are engaged here in preparing the damaged sleeping cars for transfer to Morecambe Balloon carriage sidings, on June 21 1965. The green and cream liveried camping coaches in the Hest Bank station siding, visible in the background, were a familiar landmark for many years.

Below: Raising steam at Hest Bank on June 7 1962 for the hard work ahead is Stanier 'Jubilee' No. 45633 *Aden*, awaiting the rightaway with the 9.50am Manchester Victoria-Workington (1L12). The Hest Bank water troughs are visible about 100 yards in front of the engine, starting alongside the illuminated trackside 'X' marker post which told drivers it was clear to lower the tender water scoop.

Above: The neat and tidy station at Hest Bank is the setting for this view of '5XP' 4–6–0 No. 45647 *Sturdee*, which is running south with the 8.15am Carlisle-Crewe — the famous 'Horse and Carriage' — of June 7 1962. The trailing crossover beneath the 'Jubilee' was forcibly removed by the derailment illustrated opposite and it was never replaced. The station was closed on February 3 1969, and while the down platform was removed relatively quickly and the single line track to Bare Lane was extended over its location in 1970, the up platform survived until electrification of this section of the WCML, when the lattice footbridge was also dismantled and replaced by a higher, concrete structure. The station house, on the right, is of Lancaster & Carlisle Railway origin (opened 1846) and survives today.

Below: With water pouring off the back of the overfilled tender, Glasgow Polmadie (66A) — allocated rebuilt 'Royal Scot' 4–6–0 No. 46104 *Scottish Borderer* comes off the troughs at speed at Hest Bank, heading north with the 9.35am Manchester-Glasgow of June 19 1961.

CARNFORTH

Right: Edge Hill-based Stanier '8P' No. 46229 *Duchess of Hamilton*, in far from from steam-tight condition at the front end, gets under way from Carnforth's down main line platform with the 6am Warrington-Carlisle stopping service of May 23 1963. The WCML platforms were closed from May 4 1970 and the faces cut back to permit higher speeds on Anglo-Scottish services. The Furness line platforms remain in use.

Carnforth shed yard on April 6 1962, with snowplough-fitted LNWR 'Super D' 0–8–0 No. 49449, pictured out of steam and awaiting removal of the plough. One of a class of engines introduced in 1921, No. 49449 was withdrawn from service in December 1962 and cut up for scrap at the former LYR works at Horwich in July 1963. The class, which was extinct in BR service by December 1964, was the only class in BR service not to carry smokebox numberplates. Sister engine No. 49395 is preserved on outdoor static display at the Ironbridge Gorge Museum, Blists Hill, Shropshire.

Top: An imposing portrait of the unconventional ex Franco-Crosti '9F' 2–10–0 type. No. 92024, of Kingmoor shed, stands at Carnforth (10A) on August 20 1967 in the last year of steam traction of BR metals. No. 92024, one of ten Riddles '9Fs' originally built with Crosti boilers (92020–29) and subsequently converted to conventional exhaust operation, survived in traffic until November 1967, after just 12 years service.

Above: On May 25 1964, Metro-Vick Co-Bo No. D 5705 approaches Furness & Midland Junction, Carnforth, braking for the station, with the seven-coach 10.53pm Workington-Preston (1L62). Carnforth 'bottom end yard,' visible on the right, is still in use today.

EAST TO
WENNINGTON JUNCTION

Above: Stanier '5MT' 4–6–0 No. 45228 drifts into Wennington Junction with the 2.46pm Morecambe-Leeds (via Lancaster Green Ayre) of September 20 1963. The local train from Carnforth standing in the bay platform has been brought in by the 2–6–4T just visible in the bridge arch, running back light-engine to Carnforth. This 'local' will be attached to the '5MTs' train here, and worked forward to Leeds. Note the ornate oil lamps on the platforms and on the footbridge of this station, once a busy junction, now an unmanned halt served only by Morecambe-Leeds DMUs.

Right: This was the sort of working which disappeared as the DMUs progressively entered service — a sad loss to the railway scene. On May 22 1963, Carnforth shed's Stanier 2–6–4T No. 42571 coasts the last mile towards Carnforth with the 5.43pm service from Leeds.

Mishap at Wennington Junction. In the early hours of February 18 1967, Stanier 'Black 5' 4–6–0 No. 44662 entered the down loop at Wennington Junction with a loaded coal train (the 6.15pm Hunslet-Carnforth) and was unable to stop. The '5MT' became derailed at the trap point and ran up the platform end ramp. This was the view looking east from the station footbridge later the same day: the loaded coal train has been removed, the errant 4–6–0's tender has been uncoupled and drawn clear while a pair of steam cranes (the nearer crane is from Lostock Hall shed) ease No. 44662 back towards the main line metals.

Right: Cattle grazing in the shade at Yealand are momentarily distracted by the swift passing of Stanier 'Princess Royal' 4–6–2 No. 46201 *Princess Elizabeth*, forging aggressively upgrade in charge of the 9.50am Liverpool Exchange-Glasgow of July 1 1962. This locomotive is preserved at Hereford.

Below: This was another good spot, near Yealand, to settle down with camera and notebook and the northbound bank encouraged some spectacular sights and sounds from the locomotives. On June 16 1963, Fowler 2–6–4T No. 42378 climbs steadily north with the 3.25pm service from Carnforth to Windermere.

NORTH OF CARNFORTH

Left: 'Royal Scot' 4–6–0 No. **46106** *Gordon Highlander*, fitted with unconventional straight smoke deflectors, accelerates away from the northern end of the goods lines at Burton & Holme No. 2 signal box on July 29 1962, with the very mixed stock of the 1.30pm Liverpool Exchange-Glasgow. Controlled at their southern end by Burton & Holme No. 1 signal box, these loops — almost a mile in length — were taken out of use on June 28 1971, when No. 2 signal box also closed. Burton & Holme No. 1 box survived until the commissioning of Carlisle power box in May 1973.

The 'banking' of trains is a rare practice today on BR: Manchester Victoria-Miles Platting is one of the few locations in the north west where it persists in 1986. It was much more commonplace in steam days and 'bankers' were stationed on 24-hour duty at both Oxenholme and Tebay. On September 9 1961 Fairburn 2–6–4T No. 42098 assists the 10.40am Crewe-Carlisle freight away from Oxenholme station over the double-turnout junction to Windermere. This junction was taken out of use in May 1968 and its site used in 1975 to extend the down platform.

LOW GILL — DILLICAR

Above: 'The Royal Scot' (1M22) — the 10am Glasgow-Euston of February 25 1962 is whisked south through Low Gill station, four miles south of Tebay, by English Electric Type 4 No. D 374. Located in the spectacular scenery of the Lune Gorge, Low Gill station closed on March 7 1960 and in this view workmen are busy stripping the platform edging stones. The tracks diverging to the right ran via Sedbergh and Ingleton to Clapham Junction; a passenger link which closed on February 1 1954, although periodic school specials ran to Sedbergh until September 1964. Goods traffic ceased in 1965 and track was lifted in 1967.

Right: Running through the rugged Westmorland scenery of the Lune Gorge, on the approach to the Dillicar water troughs is Stanier 'Jubilee' No. 45592 *Indore*, making good time with the 11.38pm Camden-Carlisle fast freight of June 9 1962.

Above: Standing by the trackside at Dillicar was always impressive: on June 9 1962, Bank Hall's 'Jubilee' No. 45698 *Mars* sweeps past with the scoop down on the 9.43am Liverpool Exchange-Glasgow. The sloping fellside to the right of the train is now bisected by the M6 motorway.

Below: The very attractive view from the western side of the WCML at Dillicar is the setting for this picture of rebuilt 'Royal Scot' No. 46132 *The King's Regiment Liverpool*, heading north with the 1.30pm Manchester-Glasgow (1S71) of August 6 1962. The safety valves are sizzling and the dark smoke indicates that the fireman has his engine fully prepared for the heavy task ahead, of climbing Shap Fell.

Right: Picking up water from the troughs at Dillicar is Stanier '8P' 'Pacific' No. 46224 *Princess Alexandra*, speeding south with the 10.5am Glasgow-Birmingham of March 29 1961. The leading vehicle, of GWR design, provided a through service from Glasgow to Plymouth (it was detached at Crewe) and carried an appropriate destination board. A six-wheeled milk tank brings up the rear of the train.

Below: At the same location, scoop-fitted 'EE Type 4' No. D 330 skims the troughs at Dillicar to replenish its train-heating boiler as it traverses the Lune Gorge with the 10.15am Glasgow-Euston (1M26) of March 29 1961. D 330 became No. 40 130 under the TOPS system and was withdrawn in March 1982, after 21 years service, and was broken up at Swindon Works in April 1983.

TEBAY — SHAP

Top: Viewed from the western side of the WCML just north of Tebay station, Stanier '5MT' 4–6–0 No. 45210 begins an unassisted climb of the four-mile gradient, much of it at 1 in 75, over Shap Fell. The 'Black 5' was working the 1.30pm Manchester-Carlisle of May 4 1963. The wagons on the left are standing in the former NER yard.

Above: Shap will always be remembered for its fleet of banking engines, based at the shed adjacent to the station at Tebay, at the foot of the incline. On June 9 1962, Fowler 2–6–4Ts Nos. 42424 and 42414 are standing in Tebay shed yard, ready for their next turns of banking duty to Shap Summit. Steam is billowing from the safety valves, the engines are clearly 'ready to go' and their crews will be awaiting the distant 'crowing' of a locomotive whistle from the Lune Gorge — the warning from a driver approaching Tebay that he requires assistance.

Above: Shap steam in silhouette. Tebay 2–6–4T No. 42110 assists the 10.55am Oxley-Law Junction freight away from Tebay and towards Greenholme, with three miles of climbing ahead, on May 4 1963. The three-arch brick and stone viaduct carries the main line over a Lune Tributary.

Right: Stanier '5MT' 4–6–0 No. 45344's fire is clearly in good shape as it pounds unassisted up the 1 in 75 gradient past Shap Wells on July 27 1963, with ten coaches forming a relief working from Llandudno to Glasgow (1X32).

Changing seasons at Greenholme. On March 29 1961, (top) Stanier 2–6–4T No. 42594, displaying bank engine 'target' No. 82 on the top bracket, pilots 'Jubilee' No. 45701 *Conqueror* at Greenholme with the 1.30pm Manchester-Glasgow (C400). No. 42594 was an Oxenholme bank engine which will have assisted the '5XP' through Grayrigg and will be detached at Shap Summit, to run light engine back to Oxenholme. Tebay bankers generally assisted in the rear. With winter snows lying deep on the fell, (above) 'EE' Type 4 No. D 310 disturbs the sub-zero tranquility at Greenholme as it climbs towards Scout Green with the 12 coaches of the 11.15am Birmingham-Glasgow of November 18 1962.

The 'Waverley' at Shap wells. This very unusual sighting was the result of diversions following a derailment at Stainforth Sidings, near Settle, on the Midland route to Carlisle on May 9 1963. In brilliant sunshine No. D 22 climbs unaided past Shap Wells with nine vehicles forming the 9.15am St Pancras-Edinburgh. Built by BR at Derby in 1961, D 22 became No. 45 132 under the TOPS renumbering and was still in service in early 1986.

Right: A Tebay banker at work: Fowler 2–6–4T No. 42424, in very clean condition, pushes against the Mk. 1 BSK bringing up the rear of the 1.30pm Manchester-Glasgow (1S71) of June 16 1962. The train engine had been 'Britannia' No. 70023 *Venus*.

Inset: Carlisle Upperby Fireman Billy Pearscod is clearly enjoying himself in the driving seat of Stanier '5MT' 4-6-0 No. 44678, whilst working the 2.40pm Blackpool-Paisley passenger of September 17 1962. The train was approaching Scout Green at this point.

In beautiful conditions on Shap Fell, English Electric Type 4 No. D 315, then less than two years old, climbs unassisted towards Shap Summit in charge of 13 Mk. 1 coaches comprising the 11.15am Birmingham-Glasgow of June 16 1962. After just over 21 years in traffic, this locomotive (as No. 40 115) was withdrawn in March 1982 and scrapped at Crewe Works.

CARLISLE

Right: Mid morning at Carlisle Citadel station on July 16 1962, with Horwich 'Crab' 2–6–0 No. 42834 in attendance with a short ballast train. This picture was taken in the station's carriage sidings.

Above: Unlikely though it might seem at first glance, this picture was taken at Carlisle Kingmoor shed on June 13 1964 — the occasion of a Railway Correspondence & Travel Society railtour. Taking part was Heywood 'F' class (LNER class D40) GNSR 4–4–0 No. 49 *Gordon Highlander*. Built in 1920, this engine was withdrawn from Keith shed in 1958 as BR No. 62277: it was subsequently returned to GNSR green livery and re-entered traffic for excursion duties in 1959. It was withdrawn again in 1965 and in 1966 was transferred to its current home at the Glasgow Museum of Transport.

Right: Also at Kingmoor shed on June 13 1964 was Caledonian Railway 4–2–2 No. 123 which was built for display at the International Exhibition of Industry, Science & Art, held in Edinburgh in 1886. No. 123 was subsequently used for special duties. It was withdrawn as LMS No. 14010 in 1935, restored to CR blue livery and stored at St Rollox until 1958. It was withdrawn in 1965 and in 1966 was transferred to the Glasgow Museum of Transport.

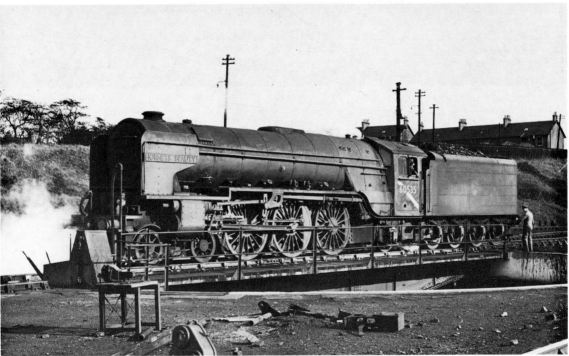

Top: Kingmoor yard yet again! Bulleid 'Merchant Navy' 4–6–2 No. 35012 *United States Lines*, cleaned to a high standard, pauses in the shed yard as another participant in the RCTS railtour of June 13 1964. A green-liveried English Electric type 1 Bo-Bo diesel-electric (now class 20) is stabled in the background. No. 35012 survived in traffic until April 1967, just over a decade after it was rebuilt in modified form. It was stored at both Nine Elms and Weymouth sheds until March 1968 and was subsequently cut up at Cashmore's Newport yard.

Above: On September 26 1964, LNER 'A2' No. 60535 *Hornets Beauty* prepares to turn at Kingmoor prior to leaving the shed and running light to Citadel station. These 'Pacifics', built with 6ft 2 in diameter driving wheels, were a 1947 development of the three-cylinder 'A2/3,' class. Worthy of note is the yellow cabside stripe, which meant that the locomotive was banned from working south of Crewe on the West Coast Main Line, under the overhead catenary wires: this was probably applied in error!

Above: On August 5 1967, Stanier '5MT' 4–6–0 No. 45279 stands in the centre road at Carlisle Citadel, waiting to take over the 9.20am St Pancras-Glasgow (1S67), whilst alongside, Riddles 'Britannia' 4–6–2 No. 70014 *Iron Duke* is in charge of 1M38, the 2pm Glasgow-Liverpool Exchange service. BR steam was nearing the end of its life at this time and the 'Britannia' is in very shabby external condition — a far cry from its gleaming days as the pride of Stewarts lane, as a regular 'Golden Arrow' engine.

Right: Carlisle Citadel station pilot, Ivatt 2–6–2T No. 41222, in very tidy condition, reverses into the platforms with milk tanks bound for Cricklewood later that day, on the 4.35pm Carlisle-Cricklewood freight. February 13 1965.

RAILS IN FURNESS

Above: Sandside, on the spur linking the FR main line at Arnside with the WCML at Hincaster Junction, was a picturesque by-way station which closed on March 1 1953, though the link remained open for freight operations until the mid 1960s. On May 21 1963 Carnforth shed's '5MT' No. 44874 runs west through Sandside with a return school special from Windermere to Lincoln.

Below: At Arnside the Lincoln-bound train shown above reversed and was worked forward by Thompson 'B1' 4–6–0 No. 61026 *Ourebi*. The train is seen here approaching Silverdale, en-route to Carnforth, where it would cross the WCML and take the MR route to Leeds.

Above: Metro-Vick Co-Bo No. D 5717 crosses the confluence of the Rivers Crake and Leven at Greenodd, on the Lakeside branch, with the 7.25pm return run of a day excursion from Birmingham to Lakeside, on June 2 1963. The first two Stanier coaches behind the locomotive are followed by a Fowler-designed vehicle. This sturdy viaduct, opened for traffic in 1869 by the Furness Railway survived closure of the branch in 1967 by more than a decade before being swept away to make room for the realigned A 590 Levens-Barrow trunk road.

The delightful setting at Newby Bridge Halt on June 17 1962 as a six-coach train formed of three twin-car DMU sets heads for the branch terminus at Lakeside, just over a mile away, with a day excursion from Liverpool. The Ford 'Popular' at the roadside was our transport for the day. You can still photograph this scene today, with steam traction at work as this section of the FR branch is now operated privately by the Lakeside & Haverthwaite Railway.

Left: On a sunny afternoon at Lakeside, Stanier 'Black 5' 4–6–0 No. 45394 awaits the rightaway with the 4.55pm departure for Morecambe (a 'Lake Windermere Cruise' service) on August 8 1965. This was in the last month of passenger operation on the branch, which closed on September 6 that year, when the Haverthwaite-Lakeside section was abandoned, but not lifted. Freight traffic survived as far as Haverthwaite until 1967, when the closure of the Backbarrow Ironworks precipitated closure of the Plumpton - Haverthwaite section. The 3½ mile Haverthwaite-Lakeside section was reopened by the L&HR in May 1973, reinstating the historic and traditional link with the Windermere steamers.

An evocative scene at Ravenglass, on the West Cumbria coast, on June 10 1962 as Ivatt '4MT' 2–6–0 No. 43028 passes time in the up loop, in readiness to work a return day excursion to Workington Main (2Z41). Known variously as 'Flying Pigs' or 'Flying Bedsteads' this class was introduced in 1947: the first withdrawals took place in 1963, although this engine survived until November 1967. It was cut up for scrap within three months, by a private contractor.

Above: On a bright, quiet morning at Bath Green Park station, 'Peak' (later class 45) diesel-electric No. D 105 awaits departure with three coaches forming the 10.10am Bath Green Park-Bristol Temple Meads service of October 21 1963. This duty became a 'fill in' turn for Midland and Northern based diesels between 'out' and 'home' trips. The station, closed in 1966 with the S&D route as a whole, has been restored as part of a Sainsbury's supermarket development.

Right: Fowler 'S&D' 7F 2–8–0 No. 53808 at Masbury Summit with the 11am down freight from Bath to Evercreech Junction, July 12 1962. Note that No. 53808, in common with its ten sister locomotives, is fitted with a tablet catcher on the right as well as the left-hand side of the tender: this facilitated the quite considerable amount of tender-first running carried out by these engines whilst on S&D freight duties. This locomotive survives in preservation at the West Somerset Railway.

Above: The southern portal of Chilcompton tunnel is the location for this picture of Riddles '4MT' 4–6–0 No. 75072, heading for Bournemouth West with the 4.21pm working from Bath Green Park on July 12 1962. The train is on the severe eight-mile climb from Radstock to Masbury Summit, and is tackling a gradient of 1 in 53 at this point.

Left: 7F 2–8–0 No. 53809 runs through Evercreech Junction on October 21 1963, pictured during a photographic visit to the Southern Region, via the S&D and Highbridge. This locomotive, now preserved in main line working order at the Midland Railway Centre, Butterley, gained notoriety on the S&D as the engine which ran out of control down the 1 in 50 gradient into Bath on November 20 1929, whilst hauling the 3.25pm Evercreech Junction-Bath freight. The 37 wagon train ran away, piling up in Bath goods yard and killing three people, including Driver Henry Jennings, and seriously injuring Fireman Maurice Pearce.

Right: On July 12 1962, the crew of '7F' 2–8–0 No. 53808 pose for the camera at Radstock North, during a brief stop with an up freight. On the left is Driver Jim Machin, from Bath Green Park shed's Goods Link, which mainly worked freights to Evercreech Junction and Templecombe on the 'S&D' and to Westerleigh Sidings and Avonmouth on the MR lines north of Bath.

Below: Shortly after the picture above was taken, Jim Machin eased open No. 53808's regulator and got under way from Radstock North with the 1.50pm up freight from Evercreech Junction to Bath. This was the return working of the 11am Bath-Evercreech Junction freight, pictured on page 60.

Ready for the rightaway at Evercreech Junction on June 11 1965 is Riddles '4' 4–6–0 No. 75072 with the 11.40am Bournemouth West-Bristol service. Alongside is Ivatt '2' 2–6–2T No. 41296, standing in the centre road (the engine spur) waiting to reverse into the platform, (after No. 75072 departs) with the 1.15pm for Highbridge. No. 75072 was one of three BR class 4 4–6–0s, allocated by the SR to Green Park for 'S&D' service in 1956. In common with all SR-based engines of its type, the 4–6–0 has a high-sided tender and double blast-pipe and chimney. In later years the WR sent more class 4s to the 'S&D,' but they were not similarly endowed.

Templecombe shed's Ivatt class 2 2–6–2T No. 41243 passes time at Highbridge on June 11 1965 with a BR Mk.1 coach and a Southern van forming the 2.20pm for Templecombe. The Highbridge branch disappeared into the history books together with the S&D itself, on March 7 1966. It was the passing of a beautiful railway which held many happy memories for me.

157

SCOTLAND

Right: With just two coaches coupled behind its tender, Ivatt class 4MT 2–6–0 No. 43139 stands at Riddings Junction, on the 'Waverley' route between Carlisle and Edinburgh, with the 3.23pm Langholm-Carlisle service of April 22 1962. Built by the North British Railway, the Langholm branch closed on June 15 1964: the NBR's 'Waverley' route itself following it into oblivion on January 6 1969.

Another vanished route from Carlisle was the Dumfries-Gatehouse of Fleet-Stranraer link, using Glasgow & South Western Railway metals. On May 15 1965 Riddles '4MT' 2–6–4T No. 80117 awaits departure from Dumfries with a pair of coaches forming the 6.20pm for Stranraer. The Dumfries-Stranraer (Challoch Junction) line was in its last weeks of life: it closed on June 14 1965. The engine had a short life: built in June 1955 it worked just 11 years before being withdrawn in March 1966, after which it was scrapped by the Motherwell Machinery & Scrap Company.

Above: A very pleasant scene at Stranraer shed (68C) on July 16 1962, with Hughes-Fowler 'Crab' 2–6–0 No. 42915 stabled out of steam, awaiting its next duty or the attentions of the fitters. Note the rounded style of the smokebox numbers, and the cabside numerals, which were bigger and lower-placed than on the LMR.

Left, above: Stranraer shed once again, on July 16 1962 with Stanier '5MT' No. 45169 keeping company with 'Jubilee' 4–6–0 No. 45691 *Orion* — the last '5XP' I needed to complete my 'set.' This shed provided motive power for the route to both Ayr and Dumfries.

Left, below: The original shed at Fort William (65J) is the setting for this study of Eastfield 'Black 5' 4–6–0 No. 44707, fitted with a snowplough for tackling winter weather on the 'West Highland extension,' on April 28 1961.

Above: On May 3 1963, Fairburn 2–6–4T No. 42693 digs in at Beattock, pushing hard against the 20-ton LMS brake van bringing up the rear of a down freight hauled by '5MT' No. 44958. The 2–6–4T is coming off the spur giving access to Beattock shed.

Right: It's a sunny day at Beattock on May 3 1963 as 'EE' Type 4 No. D 298 roars past downgrade with the up 'Royal Scot.' By this time, steam haulage of this train was virtually in the history books. The sharply curved track on the right led to Moffat, a branch closed to passengers on December 6 1954.

Above: Stanier 'Princess Royal' 'Pacific' No. 46201 *Princess Elizabeth* rolls to a stop at Stirling on July 19 1962, with the 3.50pm Perth-Broad Street fish train. In pre-Grouping days, the North British and Caledonian Railways crossed at Stirling.

Callander station on May 10 1965 with LNER 'B1' 4–6–0 No. 61347 standing at the platform with the 12pm working to Stirling. This picture was taken four months before the Callander-Killin-Crianlarich section closed (September 1965) and prior to closure of the Callander-Dunblane section, which lost its passenger service three weeks later on November 1. The 'B1' met its end in a private scrapyard in September 1967 following withdrawal from service in April of that year.

Right: Four-wheeled diesel railbuses were a convenient and economic concept, but they really came too late to save branch lines as we knew them. In this 1962 view Wickham railbus No. SC 79967 stands at Gleneagles waiting to depart as the 6.5pm to Comrie, of July 17 1962. By this time the attractive yellow 'cat whiskers' above the buffers had given way to the much larger warning panel.

Above: An idyllic scene at Killin Junction on April 27 1961 as McIntosh class 2F 0–6–0 No 57441 arrives with the 10.3am from Killin, a service which was withdrawn on September 28 1965. The official closing date was supposed to be November 1 1965, but this was brought forward following a landslide. No. 57441 was a Drummond Caledonian 'Standard Goods' type introduced in 1883, of which more than 150 examples survived in the late 1950s. This engine was withdrawn in November 1961 and was stored at Forfar for nearly a year before being scrapped privately. The class was extinct by November 1963.

Left: The Scottish country railway at Craigellachie, on the Great North of Scotland Railway system, on April 25 1961, as Park Royal four wheeled railbus No. SC 79973 waits departure as the 12.20pm Aviemore-Elgin service.

Left: The small station at St Combs was the terminus of the five-mile branch from Fraserburgh on the GNSR network. After arriving as the 10.30am from Fraserburgh, on April 26 1961, this Craven's two-car DMU awaits the rightaway for its return trip. The 'cats whiskers' below the driver's windows was altogether more attractive than the all-over yellow warning panel which came later. The Fraserburgh-St Combs link closed on May 3 1965, the Fraserburgh-Dyce Junction service lasting slightly longer, until closure on October 4 1965.

Another favourite picture which is highly evocative of Scottish steam. On June 14 1960, NBR Reid 'J37' 0–6–0s Nos. 64558 and 64608 are the subject of the fitters attentions at Inverurie works. This class of 104 engines, built primarily for freight duties between 1914 and 1921, was still intact in 1957, with examples scattered all over Scotland. Withdrawals took increasing effect from 1963, with No. 64558 being withdrawn in September 1965, while 64608 lasted until August 1966. Four examples lingered at Dundee Tay Bridge shed until 1967 but unfortunately none were preserved.

Top: NBR Holmes 0–6–0 (LNER 'J36') No. 65267 keeps company with NBR 'K' class (LNER 'D34') 'Glen' 4–4–0 No. 62479 *Glen Shiel* at Keith Junction shed (61C) on April 25 1961. Designed by Reid and introduced in 1913, the 'Glen' class consisted of 32 engines, built by 1920. Sole survivor of the class is BR No. 62469, which was restored to NBR livery as No. 256 in 1959, while still in capital stock, for excursion work. Taken out of traffic in 1965 it was moved to the Glasgow Museum of Transport the following year.

Above: Stanier '5MT' 4–6–0 No. 45497, in relatively clean condition, is turned after being serviced at Inverness shed on April 25 1961. This shed comprised a 'two-thirds' roudhouse constructed around the turntable.

Opposite: The extraordinary and ornate water tower at the Highland Railway shed at Inverness dwarfs Stanier '5MT' 4–6–0s Nos. 45475 and 45497, which are fully coaled and watered in readiness for their day's work on April 25 1961.

Right: Wick station, one of BR's most northerly outposts, on April 24 1961 with Sulzer Type 2 No. D 5131 in attendance, standing ready with the 5pm for Inverness. This locomotive had a short life: introduced in 1960 and built by BR at Derby, it was withdrawn in September 1971 without ever receiving a TOPS number. It was scrapped by BR at Glasgow in November 1971.

Caledonian Railway McIntosh '2P' 0—4—4T No. 55199 steams past Welsh's Bridge signalbox, whilst on station pilot duty at Inverness on April 25 1961. The class was in its 61st year of service and No. 55199's time was almost up at this time — the engine was taken out of traffice in July 1961 and was cut up at Inverurie Works within a month. Sister locomotive No. 55189 is preserved by the Scottish Railway Preservation Society, on the Bo'ness & Kinneil Railway.

Below: Photographs like this make you realise how much lineside equipment and atmosphere has been lost from the railways. On May 13 1964 English Electric Type 3 (later class 37) No. D 6746 waits at Firsby with the 8.44am Cleethorpes-King's Cross service. The branch diverging to the left ran to Skegness, while that to the right went to Spilsby. Note the superb semaphore signalling, of both 'somersault' and lower quadrant types, the water column and gas lamps.

EASTERN IMAGES

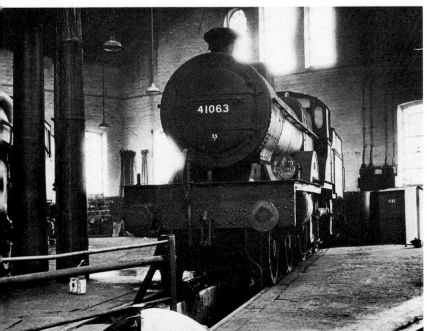

Left: A quiet sunday lunchtime at Manningham shed (55F) on February 28 1960 with LMS-built Midland 'Compound' 4-4-0 No. 41063 (introduced 1924) stabled out of use, its chimney sacked over, at its home depot. The shed is clean and tidy with a large number of fire-irons stacked in the corner of the building. No. 41063 was withdrawn later in the year, in October, and broken up at Doncaster Works in the same month.

Unusual shed-mates at Leeds Neville Hill on April 19 1964 are Gresley 'K4' 2–6–0 No. 3442 *The Great Marquess* and GER 'N7' 0–6–2T No. 69621, both stored after being privately purchased for preservation. No. 3442 (BR No. 61994) had been built in 1938 for use on the West Highland Line: it was withdrawn from service in December 1961, from Thornton shed, after which it was bought by Viscount Garnock. It is currently based on the Severn Valley Railway. No. 69621 was built in 1924 and withdrawn from Stratford in 1962, after which it was stored at Neville Hill for 11 years before transfer to the Stour Valley Railway, in Essex, where it remains today.

Shunting engines at rest at West Hartlepool shed (51C) on April 19 1964. Flanking 'J94' 0–6–0St No. 68032 are Hunslet 0–6–0 diesel-mechanical locomotives Nos. D 2586 and D 2591, behind which is stabled a second 'J94.' The 'sweep' inscription on the front of the 'J94's' saddletank was probably an instruction to the shed staff that the boiler tubes needed cleaning.

Above: The Modernisation Plan in action at Sudbury on May 11 1964, as diesel-electric No. D 5540 coasts into the station with the daily trip freight from Colchester, which includes a 20-ton LMS brake van. Introduced in July 1959, this locomotive was renumbered 31 122 and was still in service in early 1986.

Above: **Entering Gateshead shed on April 24 1960 is English Electric Type 4 No. D 245,** then just four months old, in the days before yellow warning panels of any description were applied. Note the connecting doors in the nose, the headcode indicator discs, the oil headlamp and the ladder and handhold on the 'bonnet' — all handy detail for the modeller!

Right: **Pulled up neatly to the '2-car' mark on the platform at Mablethorpe is a BR Derby green-liveried DMU set ready to depart at 10.55am for Willoughby, on May 13 1964.**

Top: The view from the down platform at Eastleigh on May 5 1961 as Maunsell 'Lord Nelson' class 4–6–0 No. 30858 *Lord Duncan* hurries past with the 'Union Castle Express,' a Southampton Ocean liner terminal-Waterloo special. Introduced in 1926, this class of 16 engines was extinct in normal service by October 1962, though class leader No. 30850 *Lord Nelson* was preserved as part of the National Collection and was allocated to Steamtown, Carnforth for main line excursion service following its restoration to working order in time for the Rainhill celebrations of 1980.

Above: This locomotive is now preserved as part of the National Collection, at York, though for static display only – it is not in working order. However, on June 10 1965 Bulleid 'Battle of Britain' class 'Pacific' No. 34051 *Winston Churchill* was being serviced at Eastleigh prior to its next duty. At this time the locomotive had just a few weeks left in service — it was withdrawn in September 1965 and stored at Salisbury (7OE) prior to preservation.

Left: USA '3F' 0–6–0T No. 30064 awaits the call at Eastleigh on June 10 1965. Built in the USA, this type was introduced in 1942 for the US Army Transportation Corps, and in 1946 the SR bought 14 examples for shunting duties at Southampton Docks. No. 30064 was withdrawn in July 1967 and stored at Salisbury (7OE) and Eastleigh (7OD) prior to private preservation on the Bluebell Railway. The engine was built in 1943 by the Vulcan Ironworks, Wilkes-Barre, Pennsylvania (works No. 4432).

An attractive array of Southern motive power at Eastleigh on July 11 1962. Locomotives on view are (right to left): Drummond LSWR '700' class 0–6–0 No. 30306, Drummond 'M7' 0–4–4T No. 30320, Maunsell 'Lord Nelson' 4–6–0 No. 30864 *Sir Martin Frobisher* and 'M7' No. 30250. No. 30306 was veteran engine indeed: the class was built in 1897, superheated between 1920 and 1927 and even in 1960 only one engine of the 30 built had been withdrawn: No. 30688 had been scrapped in 1957 following a major mishap. No. 30306 survived until April 1962. It was cut up at Eastleigh works the following month. The class was extinct by the end of the year, none of the engines being preserved.

Right: Photographed at Eastleigh on July 11 1962 (the same day as No. 92234, below) Stroudley 'AIX' 'Terrier' 0–6–0T was a stark contrast to the '9F' in terms of both size and length of service: although subsequently rebuilt, the class was first introduced in 1872. At the time this picture was taken the class was thus in its 90th year of service. Although extinct from BR service by November 1963, eight of the class survived into preservation, including No. 32678.

Riddles super-power at Eastleigh on July 11 1962. Standard class 9F 2–10–0 No. 92234 stands in the shed yard, face to face with Urie 'S15' 4–6–0 No. 30497. The '9F', built at Swindon in 1958 as part of the last class of steam locomotives ever built for BR, was less than ten years old at withdrawal in November, 1967, and scrapped. The 'S15' was rather better utilised: part of a class introduced in 1920 as a Urie development of the 'N15' class, No. 30497 was withdrawn from service in July 1963. It was stored at its home shed, Feltham (7OB), for nearly eight months before being scrapped by Cohen's, of Kettering, in March 1964.

Left: Maunsell 'U' class 2–6–0 No. 31638 hauls a westbound empty coaching stock working past Hook, a few miles east of Basingstoke, on July 9 1962.

Above: The fireman of Adams '0415' class 4–4–2T No. 30584 shovels char from the engine smokebox outside the tiny shed at Lyme Regis (a sub-shed of Exmouth Junction) prior to working the branch train back to the junction with the main line at Axminster, on June 20 1960. Originally numbering 71 engines, this class was introduced in 1882, and all but three examples had been withdrawn by 1928. All three survivors worked almost exclusively on the Lyme Regis branch in later years, until withdrawal in 1961. No. 30583 is preserved on the Bluebell Railway.

Left: No. 30584 at Lyme Regis, awaiting departure with the 3.55pm for Axminster, June 20 1960. The branch closed on November 29 1965.

Salisbury station, where the former LSWR main line was joined by the GWR metals from Westbury, was an interesting location, providing varied motive power. Here we see 'Hall' 4–6–0 No. 4905 *Barton Hall* plodding through the platforms with a train of loaded 'Oxfits' on October 23 1963. No. 4905 was withdrawn a few days after this picture was taken, being removed from capital stock in November 1963, after which it was stored at Didcot until April 1964. It was cut up by Cashmore's yard, at Great Bridge, in June 1964.

The London end of Salisbury station once again, on October 23 1963, as rebuilt Bulleid 'West Country' 4–6–2 No. 34014 *Budleigh Salterton* gets to grips with the 10.35am Cardiff–Southampton service.

Left: On July 9 1962 at Hook, rebuilt 'Merchant Navy' 4–6–2 No. 35012 *United States Lines* races West with a Waterloo-Plymouth service. This was the locomotive pictured at Carlisle Kingmoor on page 55.

Below: On July 9 1962, unrebuilt Bulleid 'West Country' 4-6-2 No. 34092 *City of Wells* sprints past Hook with a ten-coach up express, bound for Waterloo. Built at Brighton as part of the 34091-34108 batch of 1949/50, No. 34092 was withdrawn in November 1964 and stored at Salisbury (7OE) before going for scrap to Woodham's yard, Barry Docks in February 1965. It was bought by a group of Keighley & Worth Valley Railway members and moved to Haworth in October 1971 for restoration to main line operating condition. It was first steamed in 1977, officially returned to traffic in 1980 and has since done extensive mileage on both Worth Valley and BR metals.

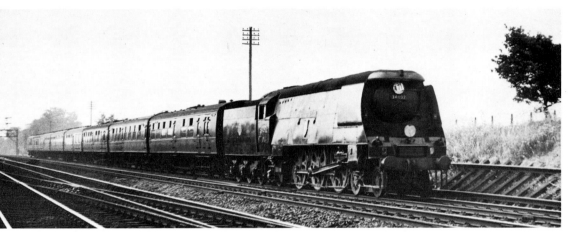

Left: LSWR Drummond 'T9' 4–4–0 No. 30120, a design dating back to 1899, has its tender tank replenished at Launceston, whilst working an afternoon Padstow-Exeter service of May 3 1961. Originally known as 'Greyhounds' for their sleek lines and sharp performances, members of the 'T9' class remained in service until December 1962, though this engine survived as part of the National Collection and is now maintained in working order on the Mid-Hants Railway.

Right: The fireman of unrebuilt Bulleid 'light Pacific' No. 34011 *Tavistock* trudges steadily at Ilfracombe as he turns his locomotive on May 4 1961 after arriving from Barnstaple on the LSWR route closed by the Western Region on October 5 1970.

LBSCR 'A1X' 'Terrier' 0–6–0T No. 32640 is serviced alongside the primitive wooden coaling stage at Hayling Island on July 10 1962, during a break in the afternoon services to Havant. Note the flat mesh spark-arrester attached to the chimney-top of No. 32640, which was built in 1878, rebuilt in 1911 and withdrawn in September 1963 after a working life of 85 years. Originally built as No. 40 *Brighton*, the 'Terrier' was sold to the Isle of Wight Central Railway in 1902 (IWCR No. 11), sub-sequently becoming SR No. W11 *Newport* and later SR No. 2640 after transfer to the mainland in 1947. After spending the last years of life allocated to Fratton (70F), Eastleigh (71A) and Brighton (75A), No. 32640 was returned to LBSCR livery following withdrawal, for sale to Butlins, for static display at the Pwllheli holiday camp. In 1973 the engine was loaned to the Wight Locomotive Society which purchased it outright in 1976, for restoration to working order.

Left: The Hayling Island branch was incredibly quaint, not least because of its 'Terrier' 0–6–0Ts. On July 10 1962 'Terrier' No. 32661 waits to leave with the 1.55pm for Havant. The Hayling Island branch closed on November 4 1963, largely because the wooden Langston Harbour bridge was life-expired. No. 32661 was taken out of service in April 1963 and scrapped at Eastleigh works the following August.

Vintage road, rail and maritime transport at Southampton Docks on July 11 1962. With the Cunard Liner *Queen Elizabeth* as a backdrop, 'USA' 0–6–0T No. 30067 runs light during yard duties, whilst the ship's crew prepare for another crossing of the Atlantic Ocean. The *Queen Elizabeth* was launched by John Brown's yard, on the Clyde, on September 27 1938, but was not fitted out until after the war, in 1946. Withdrawn from service in 1967, the ship was sold and ultimately caught fire and sank in Hong Kong harbour, in 1971. No. 30067 also survived in service until July 1967, prior to scrapping at Cashmore's yard, Newport, in February 1968.

Right: Cunard's liner *Queen Elizabeth* towers over LBSCR Billinton 'E2' 0–6–0T No. 32104 (built 1913) shunting vans on the quayside on July 11 1962. Note the twin lamps above the left-hand buffer and the train, comprised of a Gresley BG, a Southern PMV and an LMS fruit van.

Trip freight working 'Target 8' is ready to move off at Southampton Dock on July 11 1962, with 'USA' 0–6–0T No. 30072 in charge. Built in the USA by the Vulcan Iron works, Pennsylvania (works No. 4446) for the US Army Transportation Corps, the engine was bought by the SR in April 1947 and subsequently passed to BR, which withdrew it from traffic at Guildford shed in July 1967. It was subsequently stored at Salisbury from where it was bought for preservation on the Keighley & Worth Valley Railway, where it has since been converted to oil-burning operation following difficulties caused by the locomotive's shallow, flat firegrate.

GWR 'Hall' 4-6-0 No. 5917 *Westminster Hall* ambles along the down relief at Twyford, between Reading and Maidenhead, with a westbound mixed freight on July 9 1962.

Western steam on shed at Reading MPD (81D) on May 6 1961. Locomotives on view include 'Hall' 4–6–0 No. 5977 *Beckford Hall* and No. 6960 *Raveningham Hall*. No. 5977 was withdrawn from service in August 1963 and subsequently stored at this shed until May 1964 before being cut up by Cashmore's of Newport in July 1964. No. 6960 had a happier fate: withdrawn in June 1964 after just over 20 years at work it went for scrap to Woodham's of Barry, from where it was rescued in October 1972 and moved to Steamtown, Carnforth for restoration to main line working order. The 4–6–0 moved to its present home on the Severn Valley Railway in 1977.

The 'Western' diesel-hydraulics were an impressive breed, especially in the attractive maroon livery carried here by No. 1009 *Western Invader*, pictured at speed at Twyford on July 9 1962 with the 'Cornish Riviera Limited' (the 10.30am Paddington-Penzance) comprised of BR Mk.1 stock. Built by BR at Swindon and introduced in September 1962, D 1009 worked for 14 years before being withdrawn in November 1976. It languished in the Swindon scrap lines for two years before being cut up in the works in November 1978.

Above: Passing King's Sutton, between Aynho and Banbury, on July 8 1962 is GWR 'King' 4–6–0 No. 6005 *King George II* of Stafford Road shed (84A), making good time with a Paddington-Birkenhead Sunday passenger service.

Left: Steam traction by Collett, Stanier and Ivatt at Leamington shed (84D) on July 8 1962, in company with a 350hp 0–6–0 diesel shunter. The locomotives are (left to right): Collett '51 XX' 2–6–2T No. 4176, Stanier '8F' 2–8–0 No. 48264 and Ivatt 2–6–2T No. 41241, together with diesel-shunter No. D 3974. The Ivatt 2–6–2T, built in 1949 at Crewe, survives in working order on the Keighley & Worth Valley Railway.

Top: With steam billowing from its brass safety valve bonnet, Collett 'Castle' 4–6–0 No. 7004 *Eastnor Castle* is fully prepared and ready to go off-shed at Worcester (85A) on October 12 1960. The locomotive is in very clean condition, but the fireman may have been disappointed at the quality of the dusty coal, piled high on the tender.

Above: Fowler '4F' 0–6–0 No. 44553 leads an 11-vehicle empty coaching stock train into Bristol Temple Meads station on July 13 1962, in readiness for a northbound service.

182

Left: The 'Bristolian' headboard designed for a smokebox lamp bracket rather than a diesel front-end adorns the leading end of No. D 827 *Kelly* as it awaits the green flag from Bristol Temple Meads with the up working of this prestige train (the 4.15pm to Paddington) of July 13 1962. Steam was well and truly in eclipse at this time, but the diesel-hydraulics displacing Collett's 'Castles' and 'Kings' had very short lives ahead: *Kelly*, built by BR at Swindon and commissioned in October 1960 was less than 12 years old when it was withdrawn in January 1972, prior to breaking-up in the following October. In comparison, the 'Castle' and 'King' designs had both completed more than 30 years in service when they were superseded.

Roberts Riddles' 'Standard' classes for British Railways also suffered uneconomically short lives. Here we see sister Riddles class 3 2–6–2Ts Nos. 82037 and 82038, stabled between duties at Bristol St Philips Marsh MPD (82B) on July 13 1962. This shed still serves BR as an HST depot. The class 3 2–6–2T was introduced in 1952 and was extinct by mid-1967, these two engines being withdrawn simultaneously in August 1965. This class would have been perfectly suited to today's private railway operations — but none escaped the torch. No. 82007 is also visible here.

Right: During the rebuilding of the station at Shrewsbury, Hawksworth 'County' 4–6–0 No. 1024 *County of Pembroke* awaits the rightaway for Paddington with an express from Birkenhead, on April 29 1963. Rolling in on the left is Riddles '5MT' 4–6–0 No. 73025, with a train from the LNWR/GWR joint line from Craven Arms.

Collett '28XX' 2–8–0 No. 3855 stands buffer-to-buffer with '57XX' 0–6–0PT No. 9794, at Chester (GW) shed (84K) on a sunny afternoon on March 13 1960. Introduced by G.J. Churchward in 1903, this class handled heavy freight traffic over all parts of the GWR system and examples lasted into the last years of Western Region steam. No. 3855 was withdrawn in August 1965 and sold for scrap to Woodham's of Barry. In early 1986 the engine still languished at Barry Dock, although it was reported as purchased for preservation.

Above: On August 16 1961 Riddles 'Standard' '5MT' 4–6–0 No. 73049 hurries through Chirk station with an up freight. The Standard class 5 was designed at Doncaster and first built in 1951.

Left: The transitional years, when steam and diesel traction operated side by side was particularly interesting, especially at engine sheds. This was the scene at St Blazey shed (83E) on May 3 1961, with a trio of North British Type 2 diesels sharing the depot with 0–6–0PT No. 4665, and a sister engine. The large cylindrical 'tanks' flanking the turntable deck are vacuum reservoirs which powered the turntable's vacuum tractor.

BR-built diesel-hydraulic 'Warship' No. D 810 *Cockade*, constructed at Swindon in 1959, stands in the sidings at St Blazey with a china clay train for Fowey, on May 2 1961. The locomotive is painted in green livery with the later BR crest applied above the nameplate. It was taken out of traffic in December 1972 and dismantled at Swindon in September 1973.

A late afternoon Newquay-Chacewater train waits a clear road at Newquay in the charge of North British Type 2 No. D 6312 on May 2 1961. Surely one of the ugliest diesel classes to run on BR tracks, these Type 2 diesel-hydraulic locomotives were introduced from 1959 to supersede steam traction on secondary passenger and freight duties. However, the class was non-standard and had a relatively short life: No. D 6312, constructed in January 1960 was withdrawn in May 1971 and the entire class was extinct by early 1972.

Top: This is how many people will remember the British steam shed in its last days — with assorted lumps of coal, lamps, buckets, fire-irons and other debris littering the yard. In residence at Landore on April 30 1961 are (left to right): 'Castle' 4–6–0 No. 5080 *Defiant*, '56XX' 0–6–2T No. 6695, and 'Castle' 4–6–0s Nos. 5078 *Beaufort* and 4089 *Donnington Castle*. No. 5080 *Defiant* survives at the Birmingham Railway Museaum, Tyseley. Built in May 1939 and withdrawn in April 1963, the locomotive — originally named *Ogmore Castle* — was rescued from Woodham's yard at Barry Dock in August 1974.

Above: It's a sunny morning at Cardiff Canton shed (86C) on June 19 1960 as immaculately turned-out 'Castle' 4–6–0 No. 7006 *Lydford Castle* is prepared for the day's work. The 'Castle' 4–6–0, first introduced by C.B. Collett in 1923 was one of the GWR's most successful designs, and examples were still being built by British Railways after some of the earlier engines had been withdrawn. No. 7006, introduced in 1946 and subsequently fitted with a double-chimney, was withdrawn from service in December 1963 and broken up for scrap the following August, by a private contractor.

Above: A featherweight train at Clarbeston Road, where the Milford Haven and Fishguard routes converged, for Beyer-Peacock 'Hymek' Type 3 No. D 7031. The diesel-hydraulic locomotive was in charge of the single vehicle the 10.30am Fishguard-Clarbeston Road service of April 30 1963 — a sight to make the WR accountant blanch! Introduced in 1961, the class 35 'Hymek' locomotives were extinct by 1975, largely because they were non-standard. This example, introduced in April 1962, was withdrawn in May 1973 and scrapped at Swindon works in September 1975.

Right: Brecon station, April 29 1961. On the right Ivatt '2MT' 2–6–0 No. 46507 is in charge of a local service from Hereford which terminated at this station while on the left, '57XX' 0–6–0PT No. 9779 awaits departure for Neath.

A typical image of the classic GWR country railway, at Devynock, between Brecon and Neath on April 29 1961, with '57XX' 0–6–0PT No. 9779 in charge of the local passenger working, to Neath, pictured on page 94. The Brecon-Neath (Riverside) line was closed on October 15 1962.

A Rhyl-Tywyn excursion stands in the sidings at Tywyn, on August 14 1961 coupled behind the tender of Riddles 4–6–0 No. 75034, opposite the Talyllyn Railway's wharf terminus. The train is comprised principally of Stanier stock.

Ivatt '2MT' 2–6–0 No. 46504, with just two coaches coupled behind its tender, gets away from Moat Lane Junction, between Newtown and Caersws on the Shrewsbury-Aberystwyth line, with a train for Brecon on August 15 1961. With the implementation of Beeching's proposals, country railways like this vanished for ever. This route closed on December 31 1962.

Index